HOMEGROWN
Family Fun
Unplugged

HOMEGROWN
Family Fun
UNPLUGGED

JAN PIERCE, M.ED.

HOMEGROWN FAMILY FUN: UNPLUGGED

© 2016 by Jan Pierce, M.Ed.

All rights reserved. Reproduction in part or in whole is strictly forbidden without the express written consent of the publisher.

Cover and interior design by Roseanna White Designs
Cover images from Shutterstock.com

Homegrown Publications

ISBN for print: 978-0-9909764-2-4
　　　　e-book: 978-0-9909764-3-1

Homegrown Family Fun: Unplugged
An important message for today's families

Jan Pierce has addressed real concerns about children and connections. Her book *Homegrown Family Fun* is full to the brim with information and ideas on how to engage children without being plugged in. As a home educator I believe this work to be extremely useful. It could be followed as a guide for homeschooling. Jan covers everything a young family needs to be successful.

~ Mindy Lively,
homeschool parent and owner of
Home Educators Resource Directory

Homegrown Family Fun is a great book written on a vital subject with easy-to-use suggestions for parents. As an early childhood educator for more than forty years, I have seen many trends come and go. The "hurried child" trend still has its grip on modern day families, but even more detrimental to the physical and emotional well-being of children, is the influence of technology and the family's reliance on a screen to provide entertainment. Today's children are growing up ill-equipped to handle the rigors of not only childhood, but also adult life because play has lost its value. I applaud Jan Pierce for writing *Homegrown Family Fun*, which not only shares the philosophy of play, but also shows us how to make play a part of family life again.

~ Kathy Stanley,
Owner, Director and Teacher,
KIDSPACE Child Enrichment Center, Vancouver, WA

I've been waiting for a book like *Homegrown Family Fun*. I find that even when a family makes the effort to get away from it all and go hiking or camping, we still default to a movie as the entertainment of the evening. We could all benefit from more freedom from technology as our sole means of entertainment.

~ Sara Pierce Walker,
Artistic Director, McCall Children's Theater, McCall, Idaho

The thesis of *Homegrown Family Fun*, the need for unstructured play including nature play for our youngsters, is a topic very close to my heart and so needed for families today. In my thirty plus years of teaching young children we've seen an increase in disruptive and negative behavioral issues. Many factors contribute to this, but many believe limiting screen time and encouraging children to explore nature are two ways to build healthier, more relaxed and happy children. Our mothers were right when they told us to go outside and play!

~ CHERYL JOHNSON, M.ED.,
Program Coordinator, Child Development Program,
Washington State University, Vancouver, WA.

In our family we're all about unplugged fun. We like active play: swimming, hiking, biking, gardening, fixing good meals. We also enjoy quieter activities such as reading, sewing, talking, eating (and talking). In this book, Jan gives more reasons to unplug, and more ideas to make the most of family time. Enjoy this good read!

~ KYM WRIGHT,
mother of nine, author, writer,
publisher of *The Mother's Heart* magazine.

Homegrown Family Fun: Unplugged is chock-full of practical, accessible ideas to re-connect families. Jan Pierce's evidence-based wisdom, storytelling and hands-on experiences embedded in this book are a valuable resource to any family that feels something has been lost in this fast-paced world of screens and schedules. I recommend this book to my students and their families, fellow moms and anyone who interacts with children.

~ ERIN IWATA,
mother of three, and homelink elementary teacher

This one is for Elijah, Jacob, Benjamin and Ethan

Table of Contents

Chapter One..13
The Power of Creative Play

Section One: Indoor Family Fun

Chapter Two..23
The Fun and Benefits of Board Games

Chapter Three...33
Get Artsy With It: Art in Your Home

Chapter Four...45
Make Some Music

Chapter Five..52
The Importance of Family Traditions

Chapter Six..62
Creating a Literate Home

Chapter Seven...71
A Little Drama

Section Two: Outdoor Family Fun

Chapter Eight..81
Old Fashioned Outdoor Fun

Chapter Nine...91
Get Your Hands Dirty

Chapter Ten...98
Nature Walks, Field Guides and Kid Collections

Chapter Eleven..108
Treasure Hunts

Chapter Twelve..117
Mud on the Carpet

Chapter Thirteen...124
Family Projects: Lemonade Stands with a Twist

Foreword

Last week on a beautiful spring-like day, my husband and I took a walk by a nearby lake. The trees were literally full of birds and the sounds were like something out of a movie. And the smells—it had rained that morning so the grasses and trees were still damp. The sun warming leaves and blades gave off such strong aromas they took me back to my childhood when my brother and I played outdoors by the hour.

I commented to my husband that today's children probably won't build those memory banks of the sights, sounds and smells of the outdoors. They're all inside pushing buttons and watching computer-generated images. The thought made me sad.

Last winter a beautiful snowfall blanketed the Pacific Northwest—something that seldom happens here. When snow sticks to the ground, it's big news and kids can usually count on a day off school. I took a walk in the pristine, white silence.

Do you know why there was silence? Because, not a single child was out playing in that beautiful snow. No snowmen, no snow angels, no forts or snowballs. That, too, made me sad. The neighborhood children were all indoors. I envisioned them, gleeful in the snow day that allowed them to stay indoors and play more video games.

I'm not opposed to technology. I'm using my computer right now to type these words and I have websites, play online games, interact with friends online and use the instant access to information to do research for my writing. We live in a computerized world and there's no going back. There are wonderful benefits of these crazy machines.

But… there is no doubt our children are missing out on old-fashioned play. They don't need to make up games or pretend because there are countless fantastic games to play online. Aside from the fact that many of those games are violent, they consume children's thoughts and are highly addictive. If you doubt their power, try talking to a child whose eyes are glued to a screen. They're in another world.

We need to help children unplug. It's not so much that the indoor, robot-like play is so bad for them, although I believe it can be, but a bigger problem lies in the fact that we have a whole generation of children growing up without learning to appreciate the out of doors. They're not making mud pies or playing baseball with the neighborhood gang. They aren't playing kick the can or capture the flag. They aren't pretending and using their creative juices to design their own adventures.

They're missing out on learning about the trees, flowers, birds and animals all around them. They don't sit on the back porch with a dull jackknife and whittle a stick. They don't try to dig a hole to China.

And, increasingly, we have a hard time convincing children that reading books is a worthwhile experience. They don't want to join a family Monopoly game or learn how to bake cookies. Their number one choice, when given the opportunity, is to play computerized games or do computer activities.

The tricky part for parents is not only limiting screen times, but convincing children that unplugged play is actually fun. My hope for this book is that it inspires families to engage in good, old-fashioned homegrown fun. I couldn't possibly put all the great ideas for homegrown fun into one book, but if I've inspired you to search out the perfect homegrown activities just right for your family, I've accomplished my goal.

Here's to creative play and good, old-fashioned unplugged family fun.

Jan Pierce, M.Ed.

Chapter One

THE POWER OF CREATIVE PLAY

Some of you may have heard stories of life before television. Many of you remember life before computers. What in the world did people do before inanimate boxes absorbed so much family time?

Pre-technology family activities often revolved around the business of caring for and feeding the family. Daily chores without modern conveniences were time-consuming. Consequently family activities revolved around sewing clothing, preserving food, repairing equipment and the like. Those activities were satisfying and enjoyable although they were classified as work. Many of today's hobbies such as knitting, quilting and woodworking used to be necessary parts of managing a family and home.

Family entertainment a generation or two ago required few gadgets and little or no expense. When work was done, families played musical instruments and sang. They read, sometimes aloud, or told stories. Children played with homemade toys or created their own playthings. Creative play often mirrored adult tasks the children would master when they grew older.

There is a growing trend to return to the healthy, old-fashioned traditions of family life—to intentionally grow a large garden or raise a few animals so children have the benefit of learning to do chores, for example. Families work together to care for their land, and choose to enjoy family times together rather than looking outside the home for entertainment. If this lifestyle appeals to you, even in part, you'll enjoy this book.

It's no secret that today's fast-paced lifestyle leaves many of us feeling as if we're running on a never-ending treadmill. We're pressured to over-schedule, overdo and overspend. It takes a conscious effort to simplify and allow time for quiet and reflection in our adult lives.

No wonder our children mirror our overly-busy lives, often to their emotional detriment. Their days may be too full of scheduled activities to allow time for healthy, unstructured play, and play is the childhood equivalent of work. It needs to happen.

Unstructured play is the way children interact with the world around them and the way they grow in any number of social, emotional and educational skills. While some children will choose imaginative play over television or computer games, most will need a nudge in that direction.

Even educational toys have their limitations because the real need children have to create, explore, pretend and design is found in play without lots of man-made materials. They need interaction with the simplest objects such as water and cups, play dough, rice and containers. They need to play with found objects such as rocks and sticks. They need practice with imaginative play using their stuffed animals or dolls.

Plugged or Unplugged

There's good news. When given a quiet "unplugged" environment, children will enter into creative play. They'll use the props around them—household items, open-ended toys, art supplies and they'll pretend something. Children, like adults, need space in which to create. They need permission to move from an "entertain me" attitude to a "let's see what I can do on my own" attitude. While screen activities can be healthy and educational, it's a wise parent who's proactive in providing children regular quiet times for creative play.

The Benefits

Child development experts such as Piaget and Vygotsky believe that creative play is key to a child's social, emotional and cognitive development. Children learn by experience and pretend play provides a safe environment to test various scenarios found in real life.

- **Cognitive Development**

    Pretend play scenarios promote foundational understandings for future language and mathematical success. For example, the simple process of acting out "going to the store" with several different outcomes, ("Today we bought apples, yesterday, carrots") lays the foundation for children to contemplate more than one solution to a problem. And engaging in dialogue created for play characters is a certain vocabulary builder.

- **Social Development**

    When children enter into pretend play with another child, there are opportunities for growth in social skills such as taking turns or agreeing on rules. But even when a child pretends alone there are social benefits as a child directs the play of several characters, manages problems as they arise and functions as "king or queen" of the created realm.

- **Emotional Development**

    In pretend play children have the opportunity to address situations which are causing stress or fear. Perhaps your child is afraid of an upcoming visit to the doctor. Pretend playing Doctor's Office is a wonderful way to de-stress and face those fears in a safe environment—his or her own play area.

As your family life unfolds week by week, be proactive in scheduling both structured and unstructured play times. While structured activities such as music lessons or team sports have their place in a well-balanced life, our challenge today is to identify quiet spaces and protect them. There's power in your child's unstructured, unplugged, creative play.

Ways to Encourage Creativity in Your Child's Play

Here are some simple tips for creating the kind of creative play environment a young child needs.

1. **Create an Arts and Crafts Center**

    Store a variety of simple household goods and supplies to encourage creative play. These will include cardboard boxes, paper of all kinds, art materials such as crayons, markers, pencils, scissors, staplers and the like. Store play dough or a homemade version of it, fabric and old clothing and anything else that promotes artistic responses to daily life. Children love to draw after hearing a story. They love to make cards for grandparents or a sick friend. They will create their own book or design a unique piece of art for your refrigerator.

    Keep an eye open for things to add to the craft center on a regular basis. Such items might include toilet paper rolls, wallpaper samples, stamps and stamp pads, stickers, ribbon, yarn and the like. Adding a new supply to the center might encourage a new creative response.

2. **Ask Leading Questions**

    Suggest play scenarios to get your child's creative juices flowing. You might say, "Why don't you build a racetrack for your cars?" Or "What's happening at your farm today? What are the animals doing?" or "I wonder if you can make a fort with all those blankets over there?"

Creative play will tend to mirror the subjects most important to your child at a given time. Maybe you'll go through a dinosaur time period in which all stories, pretend games and art projects revolve around those big, scaly creatures. Another time the most exciting activities will relate to a holiday such as Christmas or Valentine's Day. A much-loved book might inspire hours of pretend play recreating a store or a pirate ship or a visit to the zoo.

Take your cues from your children. Whatever is in their thoughts and their words is a good prompt for creative follow up.

3. **Set the Stage**

    Take the time to be involved enough in your child's latest creative play efforts to provide the support items that encourage creative play. If she is into playing store; make some play money, gather containers, cartons and boxes. If he's into playing pilot, find a helmet, some pretend gears to shift, a cockpit made of a cardboard box, etc. When your child knows you value their creative play and will enter in at times, they'll be inspired to go a bit deeper into the pretending.

4. **Carve out Time for Creative Play**

    Most likely you'll have to limit screen time in your home to "make room" for unplugged creative play. Though there are wonderful television programs for children, there are more that are of dubious quality and influence. And though there are excellent computer games with educational value, they, too, need to be monitored. Otherwise they creep into family schedules and quietly eat up all the time.

Proactively making time for creative play will reap great benefits. Once children settle into quiet, unstructured spaces of time and have the benefit of their parents' support in engagement in creative play, they'll thoroughly enjoy themselves. They'll create characters, conflict and dialogue. They'll work out problems and design new worlds. Your walls and shelves will be filled with original pieces of art and your children will be accomplishing the tasks they were designed to do—their work, creative play.

Following is a list of suggestions for creative play stations in the home. How many others can you think of to give your children a jump-start to creative play?

1) **Doctor's office**: a play medical kit, white shirt, bandages,
2) **Post office**: supplies of papers, pencils, markers, envelopes, stickers for stamps
3) **Hair Salon**: combs, spray bottle, sheet for drape, dolls,
4) **Grocery Store**: recycled food containers, cardboard boxes, pretend food items play cash register, play money
5) **Dentist's Office**: toothbrushes, pretend toothpaste, drape, floss, dolls
6) **Restaurant**: paper and pencil for orders, pretend food, play cookware and dishes
7) **School**: books, paper and pencils, art supplies, white boards, magnetic letters, etc.
8) **Author**: paper, tape recorder, pencils, paper, stapler, stickers
9) **Veterinarian**: stuffed animals, bandages, pretend food, baskets, boxes
10) **Florist**: plastic or silk flowers, vases, jars, scissors, tape, cash register, money

For Further Study:

Books

The Hurried Child: Growing Up Too Fast Too Soon by David Elkind

Play, Dreams and Imitation in Childhood by Jean Piaget

Articles

"Play Contributes to the Full Emotional Developments of the Child," by R. J. Erickson. *Education*, Vol 105.

"The Power of Creative Play," by Cheryl Johnson, M.Ed. and Jan Pierce, M.Ed. *Momsense Magazine*, winter 2012.

"The Importance of Play in Promoting Healthy Child Development and Maintaining Strong Parent-Child Bonds" by Kenneth R. Ginsburg, MD, MSED. *AMA*, 2006.

"Problem-Solving with Young Children Using Persona Dolls," by Johnson and Pierce. *Young Children*, Nov. 2010.

"Play and Its Role in the Mental Development of the Child," by L. Vygotsky. *Social Psychology*, Vol 12.

SECTION
One

INDOOR FAMILY ACTIVITIES

Chapter Two

THE FUN AND BENEFITS OF BOARD GAMES

My parents taught my brother and me to play Monopoly and then spent the next five years finding excuses not to play the game. After all, it takes a lot of time and patience to play board games with children. They forget the rules, they may cry when they lose and sometimes they try to cheat. My brother was famous for hiding a stash of money and triumphantly uncovering it when on the verge of bankruptcy. I'm still not sure he wasn't stealing from the bank.

But there are good reasons for introducing board games to children when they're very young and continuing to play increasingly more complex games as they're ready for them. There are benefits gained in both academic skills and in social and emotional development.

The Benefits

1. **Basic Civility and Manners**

    During the life of a board game there are a number of skills that are tested and honed. Players need to help set up the game and learn the rules. They have to agree to abide by the rules and stick with the game until the end. They have to wait their turn and interact with the other players in a positive manner. And, most challenging of all, they need to be able to lose the game without negative behaviors or win graciously.

That's actually a lot to expect from children. Younger children playing with older siblings or friends often feel incompetent and outnumbered. Some children have a much lower tolerance for losing and have to struggle with their emotions—anger, feelings of failure and embarrassment. Good sportsmanship is a necessary life skill and playing board games helps develop it.

Some of the more intangible skills gained by playing games are focusing attention and developing a longer attention span, communicating clearly, waiting while others play, and managing frustration when bad luck hits. For some children these are tough assignments. If your child tends to get red in the face or cry when losing, such games provide practice in much-needed self-management.

Parents and older siblings can model positive game-playing behaviors. Another way to soften the experience for younger children is to play in teams. It's important to choose games that are age-appropriate or provide support for the younger members.

2. **Math Skills**

The simplest math board games will teach matching of pictures and numbers. They'll teach the skill of counting spaces while moving a board piece. Then they'll move on to number recognition, shape and color recognition, and sequencing. Later math board games will require operations skills—addition, subtraction, detecting patterns, analyzing probability, planning short and long-term strategies and logic.

Most math games require organization of objects, sorting by likes or differences, some will require skill in spatial relationships. Many require prediction skills.

3. **Reading and Language Skills**

   Many word games begin with simple skills such as matching, sequencing and building simple words. Letter and word recognition skills grow as children play. They must read directions to play games and be able to refer to written rules along the way. New vocabulary words will be introduced and mastered. Visual perception skills are enhanced and eye-hand dexterity builds with manipulation of game pieces.

   Word-building games such as Scrabble reinforce knowledge of the structure of words, spelling skill and manipulation of patterns found in words such as rhymes, prefixes and suffixes and root words. They encourage thought about the meaning of words.

4. **Decision Making**

   A side-effect of enjoying board games is a gradual awareness of the consequences of our decisions and choices. In games, much is accounted for by sheer luck, but as difficulty levels increase, the player must learn to make good decisions at the appropriate times. A mistake can mean a loss. Cause and effect thinking comes into play, probabilities must be considered. The player must balance risk vs. reward. Tough decisions must be made in real life. Family games are a safe place to practice making them. Parents can help guide these learning experiences by asking questions such as "Why did you make that decision? Did it work?" Reflection on past decisions is a great way to improve logic and future choices.

5. **Quality Family Time/Fun**

In our fast-paced lives, we have to be intentional about making room for family time. While movies, television and online games clamor for our free time, there is something to be said for quieter, unplugged family time. Board games offer a space of time in which to laugh, chatter with one another, eat snacks and simply enjoy being together.

Games for All Ages

There are literally thousands of board games on the market, beginning with games appropriate for toddlers and building in difficulty levels to challenge the brightest adults. Here are some board game selections in various age ranges along with the skills these games introduce and reinforce.

For Toddlers

My First Orchard, for ages 1+

Made of sturdy wooden pieces, this game teaches the skills of taking turns, rolling a die, and color recognition. It is a cooperative game in which all players try to collect the fruit in the basket before the raven can eat it.

Hello Sunshine, for ages 1+

This beginners' game comes with a beautiful stuffed sunshine plush toy. The playing cards tell mom or dad where to hide the sunshine and in the process of finding the toy, children learn relational concepts such as up, on top of, next to, inside of, etc.

Sailor Ahoy! For ages 2+

Players play this simple game as a team, trying to help Sam the Sailor reach his boat before it sails. Players will do a puzzle and build with blocks in this cooperative game.

Here Fishy, Fishy for ages 2+

Children will learn to roll a die and match colors. The goal is to catch a fish with a color matching the shake of the die. When the colors match, the player earns a piece of the puzzle.

Goodnight Moon for Ages 2-6

This game has six levels of skill beginning with simple matching of identical pictures and moving up to memory matching and finding similar objects.

For Ages Three and Up

Zingo for ages 3+

This early learning game is great fun. It is a sturdy version of a bingo card and can be played at two levels of difficulty. Pre-readers learn to match pictures and place them on their card while early readers identify sight words and play until they can yell, Zingo! Games can be played competitively or as a group until all players are winners.

The Ladybug Game for ages 3-7

This well-designed game is a winner. Kids love being one of the four color-coded characters and will learn to recognize numbers, count, recognize colors and even some words. All the while they'll pick up facts about gardens and gardening.

African Adventure Puzzle and Game for ages 4+

African Adventure by Talicor is a unique blend of game and puzzle. Join two characters who are bilingual (English and Spanish) on their journey through the jungle. Players will learn critical thinking, improve memory skills and learn jungle animal facts along the way. This game won the Creative Child Magazine Award in 2010.

More games for the 3-8 set:

Candyland, for ages 3+

This game is always a favorite because it requires no reading skills. Children move through the rainbow path past a land of candy characters on their race to the castle. The only skills required are color recognition and recognition of a few symbols. Sweet fun.

Three Little Pigs for ages 3-6

Younger children will build beginning number recognition skills and counting experience. Build your house before the Big Bad Wolf has a chance to huff and puff and blow it down!

The Sneaky, Snacky Squirrel Game for ages 3+

This game for kids three and up has a cute theme that requires players to earn acorns to feed their hungry forest friends. It builds matching and sorting skills, builds strategic thinking, hand-eye coordination and fine motor skills.

Cariboo for ages 3-6

This treasure hunting game comes with two levels of cards and teaches skill in matching letters, numbers, colors and shapes. Practice in taking turns happens when the next player receives the key to the treasure chest.

Sequence for Kids, for ages 3-7

This strategy building game requires players to play a card, place a chip on the matching character and try to build a sequence of four in a row. But watch out for the opponents' dragon card.!

Games for Ages 6-9

Wordplay for Kids for ages 6+

This excellent word building game builds skill in vocabulary, spelling and concentration. Players build words simultaneously in a series of rounds. For 2-6 players.

Dice Off: Learn Spanish for Kids for ages 7+

This award-winning travel game teaches Spanish vocabulary and grammar. Children learn on every turn, not just their own. The game cards come in four degrees of difficulty.

Bug Trails for ages 6-9

This game comes with six-legged colorful dominoes. Players learn to match colors strategically depending on whether they make a one, two or three-legged match. The game is great for color recognition, pattern recognition and simple game strategy.

Pirates vs. Pirates for ages 8+

This swashbuckling game of swords and rewards requires players to go for the gold coins while at the same time protecting their pirate. It's a great beginning game of strategy with practice in calculated risk-taking. Aaargh, Matey.

For Older Children

Ticket to Ride for ages 8-12

This train-themed game is set in the early 1900's. The goal is to build your railroad track to connect major American cities. Players learn names of cities and gain map skills. They also get a sense of American geography. This game requires strategic moves, decision-making skills and making a long-range plan. The game comes in alternate versions: Europe, Marklin (Germany), Asia, India, Nordic Countries and the Heart of Africa.

Forbidden Island for ages 10-12

This intriguing game won the Mensa Favorite Brainy Game Award for 2010. It is a game requiring cooperation and collaboration. The goal is to capture four sacred treasures before the island sinks. A complex game for older players.

The Big Fat Tomato Game for ages 10-15

Tomato farmers gear up to compete for the biggest tomato harvest. This competitive game reinforces basic math skills. Farmers work hard to grow their crop while fighting off varmints, weeds and even a dastardly Tomato Zombie.

Sounds Like a Plan for ages 10-15 and up

This is a fun game for a large group and is guaranteed to produce lots of laughter. Players match advice to a given activity. Score points if your advice is taken. Players report having a lot of fun with giving the worst advice or Grandma's advice. Great for developing the ability to think in another's point of view.

Agricola for ages 12-16

Agricola is Latin for farmer. In this highly strategic game you begin in a one-room shack and endeavor to build your farm from scratch. You may take two actions at each turn with regular turns for harvesting. What will you do first, collect stone or build fences?

Trajan for ages 12-15

Trajan is a sophisticated development game set in ancient Rome. Players try to increase their influence and power in the realms of politics, trading of goods and military domination. Made with beautiful art work and graphic design, this game won the 2012 International Gamers Award for strategy.

There are literally thousands of board games on the market. If you're looking for **award-winning** board games for your family, check out these Parent Choice winners.

Parents' Choice, established in 1978 is a non-profit guide to quality in Children's toys and games. These games have earned the Parents' Choice Awards:

- Mummy's Treasure by HABA for ages 3 and up
- Shelby's Snack Shack Game by Educational Insights for ages 4 and up
- Cat in the Hat I Can Do That by Wonder Forge for ages 4-8
- A Snail's Pace Race by Ravensburger for ages 3-5
- Gopher It! By Playroom Entertainment for ages 5 and up
- The Secret Door by Family Pastimes for ages 5-7
- Rivers, Roads and Rails by Ravensburger for ages 5-12
- Sumoku by Gamewright for ages 10 and up
- Map It! By Foxmind for ages 10 and up

- DaVinci's Challenge by Briar Patch for ages 9 and up
- 10 Days in the USA by Out of the Box for ages 10 and up
- Qwirkle, Mindware's best-selling game of all time for ages 6 and up

And, back to basics, here are the **Top Ten Classic Board Games** as judged by www.familyeducation.com:

1. Scrabble
2. Clue
3. Sorry
4. Chinese Checkers
5. Chutes and Ladders
6. The Game of Life
7. Chess
8. Monopoly
9. Twister (not exactly a board game, but lots of fun)
10. Candy Land

Sources

"Board Games for Kids: Do They Make Kids Smarter?" by Gwen Dewar, www.parentingscience.com

www.topboardgame.com

Chapter Three

GET ARTSY WITH IT: ART IN YOUR HOME

I owned color books when I was a kid and tried hard to stay inside the lines. That's about all the art I can remember happening in our home. We watched a lot of television and played outdoors a lot. (Go outside and play! And don't slam the door.) My family was a working class family and art was not on our radar. No wonder I was a bit traumatized in the eighth grade when I took a real art class and knew absolutely nothing. I still remember the teacher shouting at me, "Shade, tint, tone, don't just color in the bottle." I'd had very little opportunity as a child to explore art. I didn't know how to "see" like an artist or feel free enough to try something new and different. I didn't know how to look at a painting and find meaning. I didn't know a thing about color, line or perspective. And because I was shy and only wanted to please (stay in the lines) I didn't have the courage to strike out on my own and learn about the wonderful world of art. Your home can be different. You can choose to open all the doors to artistic experiences for your children. You can encourage artistic expression every day.

Actually the arts encompass much more than painting and drawing. Music is art. Dance is art. Drama is art. Sculpture, ceramics, baking, photography—all are a form of the arts. Any activity that allows creative expression is a form of art. There is no one right answer in art and that's a good thing for children. They can be given permission to do it their own way and create something entirely new.

In my many years as an elementary teacher I gained a great deal of respect for the learning and creativity that takes place when art materials are put into children's hands. Art appreciation classes in which children are exposed to great pieces of art, shown the subjects, the methods, materials and the strategies of famous artists and then given a chance to try something similar produced fantastic results. Children began to "see" and think like artists.

One of the most challenging students I ever had in my second grade classes positively bloomed when given time to create pieces of art. It was therapy to her. It was a chance to succeed. She created beautiful things—pieces of art I could let her share with the class and then watch her bask in the praise that she needed to hear.

Artists can be quirky folks. They tend to see the world differently, uniquely. But everyone can enjoy the arts in some form. The field is so wide, there is something just right for every child. And there's good news: not only do children love to create, it's also good for them. In the process of creating, children grow in the following ways:

Physically

When children draw with pencils and pens, paint with brushes and cut carefully with scissors, they improve their fine motor skills. They learn to move with precision. They also gain spatial awareness as they work with positioning objects on a page. They learn to see shapes in a new way and recognize patterns in works of art. They learn that objects further away look smaller and find visual relationships in figures, shapes and objects.

Brain researchers also tell us that because children spend so much time on the core subjects in their studies—math, science and reading, they need time for their right brains to develop more fully. Creative projects build connections in the right brain and allow the two hemispheres to work more efficiently together.

Socially/Emotionally

Children who are given permission to explore creatively gain self-confidence. They learn to make multiple efforts to achieve the result they want. They begin to understand there are many answers to a question—many ways to complete a given project. As they learn more about the world of art, they recognize cultural diversity in artistic expression. They learn to appreciate multiple points of view. In the performing arts children learn to work toward a group goal and to collaborate on a given project. They develop perseverance and diligence in attaining the goal. They learn to take joy in artistic endeavors.

Academically

Engaging in the arts builds and enhances language and vocabulary development. Whole new categories of words are learned in each artistic genre. And as children learn to observe and critique works of art, they'll practice critical thinking skills such as observation, description, analysis and interpretation. They'll learn to judge both their own artistic efforts, and those of others as well. They'll develop criteria for recognizing a fine work of art. Studies done by Dr. Shirley Brice Heath of Stanford University, done over a ten year period showed that children who engaged in regular after-school art classes also received better grades in school and scored higher on standardized tests. The arts are definitely a motivating force for personal growth and achievement.

Providing Access to the Arts at Home

What can you do as a parent to ensure your children have adequate access to the arts? First and foremost, make your home a "free to explore art" zone. Stock an art corner in your family room or playroom. Keep it full of engaging art supplies, books, and found objects to encourage artistic expression.

Make it a habit to talk about the art in your own home, library, church, or other public places. Visit museums or art galleries with agendas appropriate to the ages of your children. Check out books on famous artists and their works and share them at story times. And be sure to create a gallery for your child's art in a prominent place in your home.

Don't miss out on your local children's museum where the rules are always "hands on." The exhibits and activities in children's museums offer lots of opportunity for creative and dramatic play, creation of art items and a chance to engage in art, music, stories, and all manner of expressive fun.

You Can:

- Make art materials accessible
- Encourage art projects as extensions of reading, play or current interests
- Ask leading questions that lead to an art response. "Can you draw four kinds of birds?" or "How could you show me the characters in your story?"
- When possible, allow the children to see you and other adults creating interesting and beautiful things. Weave art into your daily life.

Online

Even though we're unplugging, we can't forget that online sites help us retrieve information in mere seconds. Want a recipe for playdough? Want to find a pattern for a greeting card? There's an amazing number of blogs and websites dedicated to arts and crafts in the home. These sites may come and go, but a simple web search will bring up new ones all the time. These sites offer great information on various art genres, give recipes to make your own paints and other art supplies, and often show step by step procedures to create fun projects. Want to try bathtub paint, glitter paint, puffy paint? Just look up the recipes on these blogs and websites.

www.artcuratorforkids.com

www.artwithmre.com

www.deepspacesparkle.com

www.todayscreativelife.com

www.artprojectsforkids.org

www.funart4kids.blogspot.com

www.artforyoungchildren.blogspot.com

www.redtedart.com

www.tinkerlab.com

www.smallhandsbigart.com

www.artisbasic.com

www.kidsactivitiesblog.com

www.angelaandersonart.blogspot.com

www.spiritcloth.typepad.com

www.artfulparent.com

And here are some websites with art games for children. Yes, we want kids to unplug, but there are some experiences that are worth the screen time. Art games are wonderful ways to inform children about art and give them artistic experiences. It's all about balance. You'll know when your child's eyes glaze over from too much time on any one game.

Art Detective: www.kids.tate.org.uk/games

Jackson Pollock: www.jacksonpollock.org

Picassohead: www.picassohead.com

Getty Games: www.getty.edu/gettygames

Allbright-Knox Art Games: www.kids.allbrightknox.com

The Art Zone: www.nga.gov/content/ngaweb/education/kids.html

iSketch: www.isketch.net

Architect Studio: www.flwright.org

**More Fun with Art:
Homemade Puppets = Homegrown Fun**

One of the most fun and motivating ways of self-expression for young children is to make and play with puppets. We know that creative play is the way young children learn. From babyhood on, children use their physical bodies, their imaginations, and their relationships with others as they play out stories and situations to make sense of the world around them. Pretending is the way they practice social skills, learn to express their truest feelings and fears, it's how they manage emotions and solve problems.

Puppets have always been a catalyst for creative dramatic play. Homemade puppets are even more fun because children can create their own characters. Once a puppet is made, it just begs to speak, and before you know it, you have a play! Preschool children often enjoy finger puppets and may learn to sing nursery rhymes or learn to count using them. As children grow older the puppets can be more elaborate and include button features, or glued-on hair. The sky is the limit in originality when creating puppets—they are just plain fun for kids.

Materials for puppets can be found around the house or in craft stores. (See the materials list at the end of the article) There are spoon puppets, using the bowl of the spoon for the head, paper bag puppets where the fold becomes the mouth, paper roll puppets in which a slit becomes a movable mouth, and the list goes on. There are sock puppets, paper plate puppets, popsicle stick and felt puppets. Adults can model the creation of several of these characters, but please allow children to come up with their own creations. Who cares if the dog has five legs or the dragon is orange? It's the creative process that is important. Even more importantly, it's the dramatic play that follows the creation that is the real payoff.

Once the characters are finished it's time to put them to work. Children can use them to act out well-known stories such as fairy tales or use them to recite poems. Make generic boy, girl, mom and dad puppets to act out family and friend stories. Create cartoon characters or animal characters from books to retell favorites. Create imaginary creatures with powers to fly or live a thousand years—whatever the children invent.

Now it's time to perform. All children love to perform in front of a friendly family audience. It's one of the few times they have the floor and they love it. They may have written a program for their play or maybe they've created tickets for the event. They may have added music and made props for their performance. The stage could be a table turned on its side or the back of the couch. A large cardboard box with a screen cut out works well too. It needn't be fancy—the magic of pretend will prevail. Remember to be an enthusiastic and supportive audience.

Don't be alarmed if your child's plays are filled with mock arguments and fights or if they play out fears of danger and mayhem. The drama takes them into a world where it's okay to be angry or afraid and it's safe to tell another character that they hate eating their peas. Creative dramatics is a healthy outlet for your child's emotions. Sometimes the content of their play will give you clues to inner turmoil and provide an opportunity to talk about the things that are hard to say otherwise.

Creative play is valuable to your child's social and emotional growth. It's key to his or her artistic development. It's an important part of a healthy self-concept. So set the stage for your children to have some fun. Create homemade puppets.

Puppet Creation Central: Your Craft Corner

Keep a supply of art materials and "stuff" that your kids can turn into puppets.

- Toilet paper rolls
- Cardboard
- Paper of all shapes and sizes, textures and colors
- Tape, glue, kid-friendly stapler
- Safety scissors
- Ribbon
- Yarn
- Buttons (keep away from babies and toddlers)
- Fabric pieces
- Pipe cleaners
- Paper plates
- Crayons, markers, pens and pencils
- Water paints and brushes
- Cardboard boxes, oatmeal boxes, etc.
- Paper bags
- Googly eyes

Websites with simple puppet-making information

For fabric or sock puppets go to www.familyfun.com and search for sock puppets.

For paper mache puppets try www.instructables.com and search for paper mache.

For paper plate puppet designs see www.craftsbyamanda.com and search for paper plate puppets.

For creative finger puppets see www.enchantedlearning.com and search for crafts, then puppets.

For a huge variety of simple homemade puppets you can go to www.funfamilycrafts.com/tag/puppets.

For paper plate animal puppet designs you can go to: www.dltk-kids.com/animals/paper_plates.html.

Even More Homegrown Fun: Cardboard Boxes

In this age of high tech toys and games many children have forgotten the joys of playing with found "junk". Children the world over used to play with stones, dirt, plants, and any household items that were discarded. There is something to be said for the creativity nurtured when children use their imaginations to create something out of nothing. We've all witnessed toddlers who would rather play with the wrap and ribbon than with the toy inside. Likewise, older children can have just as much fun playing with found items or using their imagination as they can with many pre-made plastic toys.

Cardboard boxes are the source of an infinite number of possibilities when it comes to creative play. Large ones can be used to create playhouses, forts, stores, schools and any other pretend building. Cut a few windows and a door and there you are, a place to play! Markers, pens, and crayons can add detail, but often just the fun of going inside and out again makes the experience real. Smaller boxes can be strung together to make trains, they can be stacked to create larger structures such as houses or stores and, again, children are delighted to play in them. Small boxes can be made into costumes, building blocks, pretend wagons, cars or boats: the ideas are endless.

A medium-sized cardboard box can be turned on its side and turned into a dollhouse with rooms, stairs, furniture and people. Hours and hours of creative play will occur as the need for each table, bed, chair and carpet spurs children on to create with their own hands.

Let me offer a word of caution as children begin to create with cardboard boxes. At the beginning of the project when cuts need to be made, parental supervision or help may be needed. If the cardboard can't be cut with regular scissors, then have an adult do the heavier cutting with a box cutter or similar tool. After that turn the kids loose to paint, color, glue and decorate to their heart's delight. Keep your eyes open for friends or neighbors who are purchasing appliances as that is a prime source of large boxes. Sometimes retail stores will allow you to carry away boxes they no longer need. It usually isn't necessary to purchase boxes, but if you want to, moving and storage businesses have them to sell.

Help your children turn on those creative juices. Gather some cardboard boxes and some art supplies and let the fun begin. You'll love the creative results.

Find Creative Craft and Play Ideas at the Following Websites and in These Craft Books

Websites (search cardboard boxes)

www.spoonful.com

www.artistshelpingchildren.org

www.parents.com/fun/arts-crafts

www.enchantedlearning.com/crafts/box

Books on Cardboard Fun

Box! Castles, Kitchens and Other Cardboard Creations for Kids by Noel MacNeal

The Cardboard Box Book: 25 Things to Make and Do with an Empty Box by Jake Danny and Niall Walsh

Cool Crafts with Cardboard and Wrapping Paper: Green Projects for Resourceful Kids by Jen Jones.

Books on Art Appreciation

The World's Greatest Paintings and Sculptures by Heather Alexander and Meredith Hamilton

Discovering Great Artists: Hand-On Art for Children in the Styles of the Great Masters by MaryAnn F. Kohl and Kim Solga

13 Artist Children Should Know by Angela Wenzel

How to Talk to Children About Art by Francoise Barbe-Gall

Books to Inspire Art in Children

The Dot by Peter H. Reynolds

Beautiful, Oops! By Barney Saltzberg
Matisse's Garden by Samantha Friedman

Emily's Blue Period by Cathleen Daly

13 Art Movements Children Should Know by Brad Finger

Ten Best American Art Museums for Kids

Each of these museums offer something special for kids. They may have kid-friendly classes, presentations or offer family tours. They will have interactive or hands-on exhibits. Be sure to visit during a not-so-busy time and take in only one major exhibit or gallery. Also be sure to take home some art—a sketch done by your child or a postcard bought from the gift shop to encourage further art study and appreciation at home. If you don't live near one of these fine museums, take the time to check out your local museums. Many of them have wonderful presentations offered with children in mind.

1. Art Institute of Chicago
2. Metropolitan Museum of Art, New York City
3. Dayton Art Institute, Dayton, Ohio
4. DeYoung Fine Art Museums, San Francisco, California
5. Carnegie Museum of Art, Pittsburgh, Pennsylvania
6. Los Angeles County Museum of Art, Los Angeles, California
7. Joslyn Art Museum of Omaha, Omaha, Nebraska
8. Winterthur Museum and Country Estate, Winterthur, Delaware
9. Dallas Museum of Art, Dallas, Texas
10. Peabody-Essex Museum, Salem Massachusetts

Chapter Four

MAKE SOME MUSIC

Music Lessons?
Your Child's Brain Will Thank You

Are you interested in building your child's brain power? Over the last decade brain research has determined that children who take music lessons show improved brain development with increased memory capacity. The studies also show higher general intelligence in skills related to language and reading, mathematics and overall IQ scores. Dr. Peter Simon, President of the Royal Conservatory of Music in Toronto, Canada says, "Music education is a powerful tool for attaining your child's full intellectual, social and creative potential." The test results are enough to make you a believer.

Even in the best of times it may be difficult to find funds for extras such as music lessons. But the facts concerning the benefits of regular music instruction on your child's brain development make a very strong argument for including them. Further, the earlier you begin exposing your child to music, the better the results will be.

There's no magic here. Neuroscientists have teamed with educators to test young children's brain development and have made remarkable discoveries. Music study requires precision in auditory (hearing) processes, multi-tasking, such as hearing and reading notes simultaneously, and focused attention to the task. Not only do these activities aid in earlier, stronger brain development, but decades later adults who studied music show quicker and more accurate responses to sound patterns.

What does this mean? MRI's and other imaging devices show when a child's brain is exposed to regular sessions of music study, it builds increased white matter made up of nerve fibers which serve as connectors between motor regions of the right and left hemispheres of the brain. In other words, the brain builds a structure on which new skills can grow, and that structure lasts a lifetime.

The Benefits

- **Music education can improve speech and reading ability.**

  Musically trained children have shown increased ability in phonological skills, (identifying where syllables and words begin and end) which aid in learning one's own language and new ones.

- **Music education can improve basic memory skills.**

  Studies show musically trained individuals develop better working memories. A working memory allows us to remember things even while our minds are busy with another task—a crucial skill for problem solving in math and comprehension in reading.

- **Music exposure builds creativity, empathy and social awareness.**

  Neuroscientists have found increased communication between the two sides of the brain in musically trained children, believed to increase creativity. Tests show participating in collaborative music-making, increases empathy for others. This may be due to increased verbal intelligence by which a child picks up nuances of speech and the emotions behind them. Making music requires cooperation and focused attention which are valuable skills in personal relationships.

- **A study done in 2007 showed increased test scores for students having had quality music instruction.**

   Whether music exposure was received in the home, in a group or individual settings, a quality experience with music instruction was key to higher test scores in English and Math. (Christopher Johnson, Professor of Music, University of Kansas.)

- **Music training is beginning to show increased health and well-being into old age.**

   Studies are emerging which show music training provides improved cognitive function all through life. Music therapy is helpful to those recovering from strokes, those who stutter or have other neurological problems and those with autism and Parkinson's disease. It is believed to help delay the onset of dementia.

   The resources and efforts expended in providing musical training for your young children will deliver lifelong benefits. That training leads to lasting, positive brain changes. It increases capacity to perform tasks requiring sustained attention, careful listening and engaged reading. Finally, music training builds creativity, encourages empathy for others and builds a healthy sense of self-confidence.

Right from the Start

We know that babies in the womb are able to hear and respond to sound. Why not begin your child's musical appreciation right from the beginning? Listen to a variety of musical genres. Include classical, folk, jazz, blues and silly songs. Choose a time of day to respond to music of one kind or another. You might include soothing songs before naptime. Silly songs before going outside to play or choose to move and dance to favorite pieces before settling down to study times.

While children enjoy music made especially for them such as the Raffi or Dan Zanes CD's, music is one area of learning and expression where "one size fits all." The youngest child can learn to appreciate classical music and select favorites. The key is exposure. The more kinds and varieties of music you bring into your home, the broader your child's musical appreciation.

Family Jam

Whether you're having a singalong in the car or around a campfire, or playing homemade instruments along with a piece of music, you'll inspire your children to become music-makers if you include family musical times in your schedule.

Many times children associate music only with a formal lesson and that dreaded practice time. And, yes, practice is very important to master any new skill. But if the family has already spent a lot of fun time enjoying music together, your children will have the motivation necessary when they're old enough to select an instrument, absorb skills during the lessons and take the initiative to practice and get better at making their own music.

Another piece of good news is that you can find excellent online music lessons for a variety of instruments including guitar, harmonica, flute and recorder. These online lessons remove one of the biggest barriers to learning to play an instrument—the cost of hiring a teacher. And another way to minimize expenses it to rent instruments or find them at a reduced price online.

You might decide that everyone in the family is a musician of sorts. Wouldn't it be fun to make music together on a regular basis, even if the instruments are a kazoo and a tambourine? Children naturally enjoy music and you can promote their appreciation of it in so many ways.

Simple Musical Instruments You or Your Children Can Make

Toddlers and preschool children love to use simple rhythm instruments to play along with their favorite songs. These instruments are simply made from art supplies and objects you can find around the house.

Some easy choices are: jingle bells on sticks, simple tambourines, "rain sticks", coffee can or oatmeal box drums, shakers made from a closed container with beans or rice inside, maracas from balloons and flour paste or gourds, or castanets made from folded cardboard strips plus bottle caps.

To find directions for making these and a whole host of other homemade musical instruments see:

www.atozhomeschooling.com
www.kinderart.com
www.redtedart.com

Exposure to Great Music at Home

If music is already a part of everyday life in your home, it's a simple step to become a bit more proactive in selecting the pieces you introduce. Begin with familiar songs such as nursery rhyme songs or familiar movie scores and move up to kid-friendly classical pieces such as Peter and the Wolf by Prokofiev or Carnival of the Animals by Saint Saens. Most recordings of child-friendly classical music come with simple lesson plans.

Music educators tell us that children can learn more about music from listening to orchestral music which changes in pitch, pace, key, etc. more often than other performing groups. And children gain experience in recognition of the sounds of various instruments—the horns, the strings and percussion.

Build a musical library at home, or make use of your local library to include a wide variety of offerings. Listening to music from other cultures is another way to broaden your child's music appreciation skills.

Music is truly the universal language—children of all ages are enriched by listening, appreciating and diving in to make their own beautiful sounds.

For a list of songs to teach music appreciation skills go to www.songsforteaching.com and click on music appreciation.

In the Community

Many school districts have music appreciation assemblies in addition to their regular music classes. Children will hear the local orchestra or choral groups, they'll get an introduction to opera and perhaps hear small groups such as string quartets, pop groups, barbershop quartets and the like.

Your community has a variety of musical presentations throughout the year. The Christmas season is a great time to hear orchestra and choral presentations as are the summer months when outdoor concerts are popular.

Make it a habit to attend local high school and college musical presentations. Whether the offering is a musical or a program of classical offerings, your children will know that you appreciate the world of music and they can too.

"Older Adults Benefit from Music Training Early in Life" by Nina Kraus, PhD. *Journal of Neuroscience*, Nov. 5, 2013.

"Music Lessons Early in Life Could Boost Brain Development" by Lily Avnet. *The Huffington Post*, Feb. 18, 2013.

"Those Piano Lessons Will Keep You Sharp in your Old Age" by Tom Jacobs. *Pacific Standard*, Nov. 7, 2013.

"Five Amazing Benefits of Exposing Young Children to Music Instruction," EarlyEducationEssentials.com.

"Early Musical Training and White-Matter Plasticity" by Christopher Steele, et al. *Journal of Neuroscience*, Jan. 16, 2013.

"First Evidence that Musical Training Affects Brain Development in Young Children," *Oxford University Press*, Sept. 20, 2006.

"The Benefits of Music Education: Your Child's Development: Music Study may be the Best Tool," *The Royal Conservatory*, April 2014.

Further Reading

This is Your Brain on Music by Daniel Levitin

Music, Language and the Brain by Aniruddh Patel

"Short-Term Music Training Enhances Verbal Intelligence and Executive Function," by Sylvain Moreno, et al, *Psychological Science*, Oct. 3, 2011

"Why Music Makes our Brain Sing," *The New York Times*, June 9, 2013.

"Early Music Lessons Have Longtime Benefits," *The New York Times*, Sept. 9, 2012.

Chapter Five

The Importance of Family Tradition

What is your family's story? What is your identity? If you had to answer those questions in one paragraph, what would you write?

Do you define your identity in terms of faith? Location? Vocation? Recreation? Who are you and how does each person in your family fill a certain position in the family tree? I don't mean just first born or youngest, I mean who are you in terms of your purposes and your dreams? What are you trying to accomplish as you raise your family?

What are the deepest-held beliefs that guide you as you make decisions about what you teach your children and how you spend your time? What kind of adults do you want your children to become?

These are weighty questions and ones we may gloss over in the middle of our busy schedules. But if you're reading this book, you probably want your children to enjoy the best of everything. You want them to be people of character, able to live well and do good to those around them.

Some of the ways we can foster positive character traits in our children come through family identity—the stories your family pass on through the generations and the way each member of the family thinks about "his or her people."

Stories are Powerful

When my children were young, nothing got their attention faster than my husband or me telling a story from our own childhood. They loved to hear how things were different in our day or what we did for fun. They especially liked the stories that told of our less-than-perfect young lives. And if we **really** wanted them to learn a lesson, we simply told each other a story about the value of telling the truth or being respectful to others or some other nugget of truth. The kids just eavesdropped their way to becoming better citizens.

Stories are powerful. Stories showcase characters in some sort of dramatic action. They have adventures, problems to solve, heroes to save the day or scoundrels to catch and set aright. Stories are fun. Don't forget that the senior members of your family have stories to tell your family as well. I remember my Dad, who grew up on a farm, telling of how my Uncle Leslie locked his Ma in the chicken house and proudly said, "We sure have a big hen in there today!" All those stories of how hard kids worked in the olden days may elicit yawns, but how about the stories of times you struggled in school and then succeeded? How about the times you were either wonderful or horrible at a certain sport? Is it sad or funny, scary or silly? If it is, then it's a story. You need to tell it to your children.

"Publish" Your Family Stories

Reading and writing are eternally connected to one another. In learning, both skills are highly valued. Why don't you sit down with your kids and write one of your family stories together? Perhaps you can talk and he or she can write down the main ideas. Then together you can flesh it out, being sure to place the right emphasis on the funny or hair-raising parts. You can add original illustrations, bind it and keep it forever. Or you can put your stories on tape recordings or CD's for future enjoyment. A family friend, a wonderful 91 year old who went sledding down her great-grandchildren's driveway last winter, has written her memoirs of raising five children. It was a special edition written only for them and they treasure it. This great grandma has no college degree; she just has a life filled with all the joys and sorrows of real life.

Sit down and think. Where did you live? Where did you go to school? Who were your friends and why? What were your parents and grandparents like and what is there to tell about their lives? What adventures did you have or imagine as a child? What was hard for you, easy for you, challenging for you, fun for you? Did you spend your days reading books or working in fields? Did you have overseas military service? Did you have a job that your children may not know about? The possibilities are endless because life itself is interesting to your own family members. Jot down some notes. You may find yourself digging up memories you had long forgotten. Tell your stories, they are pure gold.

Family Holiday Traditions

Holidays often brings about feelings of nostalgia. Why? Because we've all enjoyed family traditions over the years and wish to pass them on to our children and grandchildren. Have you ever wondered why people love holiday television ads that hearken back to years when teams of horses pulled carriages across snow-covered fields to Grandma's house? It's not that we ever really did that, but the fact that it used to happen and it sure would have been fun. It would have been a happy family tradition.

We love traditions for a number of reasons:
1. **Traditions provide family identity.** Maybe your family always drives to the mountains to cut a Christmas tree.

Or maybe you always eat clam chowder on Christmas Eve. Maybe your children play the dreidel game and you eat potato latkes. Such activities provide a strong sense of family identity.

2. **Traditions strengthen family bonds.** Children love to help bake and decorate cookies. They love putting decorations on the Christmas tree. They look forward to the family gatherings that will occur over the holidays. Doing these activities builds connections between family members.

3. **Traditions offer a sense of security and belonging.** "This is what we do." Traditional activities connect the generations and stories of "how it used to be" are always welcome. Children will enjoy the feeling of belonging to this particular group of people called family.

4. **Traditions offer a time to teach family values.** Do you help feed the homeless or give toys for foster children? Does your family make it a priority to send gifts to the poor in other countries? Do you look for a way to bless others in a time of celebration and plenty? Your children will notice and make that a personal value in the future.

5. **Traditions make wonderful memories.** Perhaps the most important thing we can do as families is create warm, positive memories of times together. Families aren't perfect, but at holiday gatherings they can come close—they can share fun, festive times together to remember for many years to come.

What are your holiday traditions?

Maybe it's time to reinforce traditions that have gone by the wayside or create some new ones. A new tradition can be set in just a year or two in the lives of young children. Here are some ideas for fun activities that can become your family traditions:

Thanksgiving and Christmas

Most Americans hold these two holidays dear to our hearts. We gather the memories from our growing-up years and try to reproduce them as adults with our own families.

- Plan a time dedicated to the Christmas tree. Whether you cut your own or go to buy one, the act of buying, setting up, decorating and then enjoying the magical ambience of the beauty is a memorable tradition. Maybe you want to have a separate, tiny tree especially for the children to decorate.

- Baking goodies together is memory-making. Is there a recipe you make every year? Are there treats you make to give to friends and neighbors? Do you use some of the baked items as decorations around the house?

- Music. Everyone has their favorite Christmas songs. Or maybe your family always goes caroling or to a certain Christmas concert. Music lifts the spirits and calms the most troubled heart.

- Cards and letters. This tradition is becoming old fashioned for many reasons. But a hand-written message of love and joy at the holidays is always welcome, especially to your elderly family members.

- Gifts. We do tend to overspend during the holidays. Remember a gift is meant to please the recipient in a special way because it's chosen with love. Simple gifts can be the most important ones.

- Movies. There is a wonderful assortment of family Christmas movies to enjoy together.

- Sports events. Many families enjoy their loyalty to one sports team or another. While these traditions are not only for the holidays, they can be fun and exciting for younger family members as well as the oldsters.

- Traditions of faith. The holiday season is a time where we're looking for our roots. What does your family believe and how do you incorporate that into family times together? Sharing faith with the extended family can be a precious time filled with good memories.
- What other holidays does your family celebrate? Do you make a huge deal over birthdays, Valentine's Day? Mother's or Father's Day? Easter? Whatever you take the time to make special will become a family tradition. Those traditions are valuable.

You may have friends who celebrate Hanukkah (Chanukkah), the Jewish holiday commemorating the rededication of the Temple in Jerusalem. It is an eight day celebration with highlights including lighting the candles of the menorah, playing dreidel, a game with a four-sided top, and eating special foods such as potato latkes.

You may want to find books on holidays celebrated all around the world to help your children understand that holidays and celebrations are a part of every culture. Some holidays to explore might include Diwali, the Hindu Festival of Lights in India, Las Posadas, the nine day Mexican celebration of Jesus' birth in Bethlehem, Kwanzaa, a seven day celebration of African heritage and culture, Chinese New Year with its dragon parades and special dishes or Ramadan, the Muslim holy month. Here are a few books to inform your family on celebrations around the world.

Holidays Around the World Series by Deborah Heiligman
Children Just Like Me by Anabel Kindersley
Holiday Series by Carolyn Otto

We all long for a sense of purpose. Who are we and what do

we hold dear? Holidays are times to go beyond the ordinary—times to leave the day to day rhythm of work and chores. Holidays fill our need to celebrate and family traditions will enrich your family's lives for generations to come.

From Family Stories to Biographies and Autobiographies

Biographies and autobiographies, stories of real-life people, are powerful tools to engage your children. Boys especially love stories that tell about the real and true. It used to be that children's literature was all about fiction. We started early readers out with nursery rhymes, moved on to fairy tales and folk tales, then picture books and finally on to the very prestigious chapter books. There wasn't a non-fiction book in sight. Then educators began to realize that much, if not most of adult reading is about real things. We have to read street signs and contracts, we fill out job applications and follow directions to assemble new play structures. Teachers began to ask school librarians to order books about animals, machines, space and how car engines work. Publishers got on board and began to print good non-fiction books about everything real in the world. And biographies and autobiographies were written on thousands of interesting and important people from all around the world. Finally, there was a balance for children in their reading choices. They developed a taste for both fiction and non-fiction. And, as a bonus, struggling readers, especially boys, began reading for pleasure.

Once non-fiction books became readily available, then reading strategies for non-fiction material had to be taught. In a fiction story the words just keep coming. But in non-fiction it's important to know about illustrations, captions, headings, indexes, maps, blow-ups of pictures, labels and much more. There is an art to reading non-fiction. It's a doorway into the real world.

Biographies meld the best of narrative writing and non-fiction with all of its intricacies. A good biography telling the life story of a human being is full of drama. Its merits often lie in real-life triumphs over poverty or the hardships and dangers of war, in hard decisions that made all the difference, or the courage to face adversity. Real-life dramas are at the heart of a well-written biography.

In addition to the interest of a real-life story, when children read a biography they're learning about positive character traits they may incorporate into their own lives one day. They're getting a sense of history and timelines. They're beginning to understand what the world was like in a given place at a given time. They'll learn that life is not static, that the world is ever-changing. Biographies are wonderful for developing the skills of reading comprehension. The story is motivating—the reader wants to understand and stays engaged. He wants to know what happens next in the character's life and she wants to understand why the main character lived in a particular way.

Another plus in choosing to read biographies is the broad array of choices. Select from the lives of kings and queens, explorers, scientists, great artists, sports figures, Native American chiefs—the list goes on and on. There are biographical series written about both historical and contemporary figures. Name any topic you can imagine and there is a leading figure whose life story will influence readers.

Biographies lend themselves to publication in sets or series. Thus you will find such offerings as the **Young Patriot Series** in American History, or the **Blue Banner Biography Series** by Anne Graham Gaines on current world figures. Certain authors such as David Adler are well-known for their biographies written for children. **The Lifetime Series** by Thameside Press in the UK has a wonderful series of world figures such as Nelson Mandela and Anne Frank. Heinemann has published a series on famous artists with titles such as **The Life and Work of Mary Cassatt**, and Rourke has a series called **People Who Made a Difference**. Other series tell the life stories of authors, scientists, astronauts, poets and playwrights and virtually any group of people in which your child may develop an interest.

One way to whet your child's appetite for biographies is to track their current interests or their current courses of study and then supply just the right title for the time. If they're learning to use the microscope in Biology class, they may be interested in the life of Van Loewenhook or Madame Curie. If they're studying India in geography they may be interested in reading about Mother Teresa and her work with the poor and dying of Calcutta. If they take a fancy to the American Civil War, then a biography of one of the leading generals is the right choice.

No need for history to be a dull course filled with endless memorization of dates and places. Bring the character and his or her life to life with a biography written at the appropriate reading level for your child. Look at these biography series to search for the perfect title for your young reader or browse your local library or bookstore for the right book.

Early Readers

Tomie de Paola's books such as *Nana Upstairs & Nana Downstairs* or *26 Fairmount Avenue.*

Let's Read About Series by Scholastic with biographies on such characters as *Cesar Chavez* and *Pocahontas.*

The Childhood of Famous Americans Series by Aladdin with biographies of Daniel Boone and Helen Keller and many more.

Picture Book Biographies by David Adler. These lovely books combine pictures and easy text to tell the stories of people such as Sojourner Truth and Thomas Jefferson.

Middle Grade Readers

The Who Was Series by Grosset and Dunlap has titles such as Who was Thomas Edison and Who Was Leonardo da Vinci. Written for grades 3-7

Legends in Sports by Matt Christopher tells the life stories of sports legends such as Michael Jordan, LeBron James and Peyton and Eli Manning. For grades 3-5

The Time for Kids Biography Series by Harper Collins are for children 6-10 and tell the stories of historic characters such as Clara Barton and Jesse Owens.

Tweens and Teens

Biography for Beginners studies the lives of famous philosophers, mathematicians and scientists such as Marx, Foucault, Heidegger and more.

DK Biography Series are written for ages ten and older and chronicle the lives of historic figures such as Albert Einstein, Mahatma Gandhi and Marie Curie.

The Avisson Young Adult Series tells the stories of interesting Americans such as Eleanor Roosevelt and Audie Murphy.

Chapter Six

Creating a Literate Home

It's virtually impossible for a former teacher and reading specialist to write about family fun without addressing a supportive environment for reading and writing. If your children can read well, they can learn anything. Not every child will want to spend part of their free time reading, but I hope yours will. And if you provide materials and positive vibes when it comes to literacy and all it offers, you'll increase that likelihood.

A literate home supplies books or the means to borrow them, and lots of writing supplies. The craft corner you keep for art projects can double as a writing center. Horde all the paper products you find and keep pencils, pens, markers and the like readily available. You never know when your children will want to write a letter or poem or jot down a story running through their heads. When your children are pre-school age, be sure to have letter magnets and alphabet blocks available for recognition and for word making. And, it's vitally important that your children see you do a lot of reading and writing too. Modeling a love of words and books and all things literate is the most powerful tool you have for encouraging literate children.

Jan Pierce, M.Ed.

What is a Literate Home?
The Importance of Talk

Good parents know they should read to their children. It's the right thing to do to help them gain reading readiness skills. But did you know that talking to children is equally important in getting them ready for learning? It's true. Talking to children from the day they're born and gradually leading them into two way conversations about their everyday world can mean the difference between success and failure in learning.

My husband and I both grew up in lower middle class families. Children were loved, but expected to stay quiet during adult conversation. And, the conversations were mainly about practical things like the work to be done or what we'd watch on television that night. When our parents spoke to us the words were usually directive, as in "Eat your peas" or "Don't hit your sister."

Luckily for my husband, he lived with his elementary teacher grandmother for the first ten years of his life. She did all the right things: she fed him good, nutritious food, taught him correct grammar and instilled in him a love for learning about the world—the stars, trees, flowers, birds, animals and more. She shared her knowledge with him and never stopped believing in him even though he was a "late bloomer" in school. She took the time to talk with him.

And me. Thank God, my mother was a talker. My father was a quiet man, but my mother more than made up for that. She didn't speak to my brother and me with the expectation of hearing our responses, but at least she talked a blue streak and we learned a lot of vocabulary. She had a sense of humor that lent itself to plays on words. She wrote little poems for office parties and family gatherings. She was a verbal whiz. In turn, I learned to love words.

So what, exactly, is the ideal home environment for later learning successes? Studies on key elements in children who learn quickly and do well in school clearly show that a home rich in talk is one of the essentials to later learning. Interestingly, the number of words spoken to children in a home increases with socio-economic status. The higher the education level of the parents, the more they engage in speaking to their children. And the quality of the language is higher, moving from only directive or disciplinary words to asking questions and talking about feelings, thoughts, goals, and relationships.

A landmark study begun in the 1960's at the University of Kansas conducted by Todd Risely and Betty Hart uncovered remarkable information about the talk/learning connection. This team tracked 42 families by taping conversation in their homes an hour a month for two and a half years. The results were surprising. Low income children heard an average of 600 words per hour, working class children heard about 1200 and the children of professionals heard approximately 2100 words per hour. By age three the poorer children had heard thirty million fewer words than wealthier children.

What made this study so important was not just the initial tracking of language spoken in the home, but the later follow-ups on these children and their performance in school. The children from language-rich homes were more successful learners, and scored higher on IQ tests. The exciting thing was that when a lower income home **did** record more talking to children, those children also scored higher and did better in school. That's good news because talk is free.

In Providence, Rhode Island a group of city caseworkers has taken the information in the Risely and Hart study and given it feet. They've made home visits and added "conversation services" to their agenda. They provide recording devices to families and encourage them to speak more to their children. With practice, the quantity and the quality of parent/child interactions has increased. Parents are taught to praise their children and to respond to the child's language with more information, (Doggy? Yes, that's a brown doggy.) and generally raise the number of verbal interactions throughout the day.

What does all this information mean for your home learning environment? You can give your child a boost in language learning. Much of the language experience can take place while reading to your child. Books lend themselves to many forms of language experience and you can begin the day your baby is born. Singing songs, reciting nursery rhymes, engaging in word games such as How Big is Baby? Soooo Big, all of these provide rich learning for your child.

Talk to your child throughout the day. With older children make it a point to ask questions that are open-ended. What is your favorite color? Why are you feeling happy, angry, afraid? What was the best thing that happened today? Take opportunity to praise your child appropriately. (You're right, that is a dinosaur. Can you find another one?) You respond to their speech and add a bit more.

If you grew up in a home that didn't do a lot of talking, you might find it a stretch to add to the number of words spoken to your children. But know that words are free and you are doing a wonderful service to your child's language awareness and future learning success. So talk, talk, talk—your child will benefit from it.

Fast Facts on Children and Language:

- Families tend to talk more to girls than to boys which may account for language delays in boys
- Even babies benefit from lots of talk. They learn vocabulary, begin to identify objects, respond to various emotions and relationships.
- Children who are "talk deprived" will have a smaller vocabulary and test lower on language processing skills tests.
- Children love repetition in language. It helps them remember words and learn the relationships between

them.
- The gap between language rich and language poor homes can cause a child to be as much as two years behind in language skills when they begin school.
- Television or other "electronic" language is not helpful to a child's language growth and can even be a detriment as it blocks out real communication with family members.
- Learning potential can be either optimized or stunted. As Erika Hoff, a developmental psychologist from Florida Atlantic University put it, "Children cannot learn what they don't hear."

The Importance of Good Listening Skills

In addition to speaking an ever-increasing number of words, children also need to be able to listen carefully to take in necessary information. A child who can't attend at the proper times is likely to do careless work and miss important pieces of information.

More than Just Hearing

Focused listening is one of the most important skills your child will ever learn. Children with strong listening skills do better in school, sports, relationships and eventually in their careers. But many children lack this important skill and parents are rightly concerned. What can you do?

First, listening is much more than just hearing. It is a given that you will have your child's hearing checked by medical professionals and follow up with any problems discovered. Occasionally a wax build-up, ear infection, fluid behind the eardrum or other relatively minor ear problems must be addressed. If your child does have a hearing loss, be very sure to do all you can to maximize his or her hearing.

But listening problems are a different issue. *"Listening is the conscious process of receiving meaning from the sounds we hear. It implies the ability to stay focused on the message, screen out distractions and make a meaningful connection with the content of the message. Good listening requires practice because it requires effort to do it well."*[1]

You can see that good listening requires not only the ears, but engagement of the mind and body as well. It is a series of decisions made by the listener and it can break down quite easily. Even children who want to "pay attention" and "follow directions" may be unable to if their attention is pulled away by background noise, movement, or other competing thoughts and sounds. Children need practice in focusing their attention, receiving the message, understanding the message and then responding in the appropriate way.

Practice Makes Perfect

You can help your child become a better listener. Here are some simple ways to build active listening skills.

- **Model active listening**. Build listening motivation and success by intentionally gaining your child's attention before expecting him to listen. Whenever possible, make eye contact before speaking. When he responds, maintain eye contact and repeat the content of the message or model good listening by using appropriate body language such as nodding.

- **Encourage conversations** on topics of her choice. Model good listening and show your appreciation for her ideas. It is surprising how little conversation takes place in our daily lives with today's busy schedules. Mealtimes are often good times to engage in conversation.

---

[1] "Helping Kids with Learning Disabilities Build Listening Skills" by Dr. Kari Miller. *L.A. Special Education Examiner,* March 11, 2011.

- **Read to him every day.** A ten to fifteen minute read aloud session is one of the most powerful strategies you have to build listening skills. Select books he enjoys and stop often to predict what will happen next or to ask his opinion about the action in the story.

- **Build her inner language** by having her repeat back what you've said to her. Or ask her to explain what she is doing or what she plans to do. This will help her to focus on the steps in the process and will help her with listening to receive information and follow steps sequentially.

- **Do the peanut butter and jelly sandwich game.** Ask him to write down the directions for making a pbj and then you model following those directions *exactly*. Chances are there will be some gaps in the directions which make for a funny and a bit messy activity. The point will be made: listening and following directions is an exact skill if you want a good end product.

- **Play the "add one more" game.** Give one direction such as "Touch your nose." Then add a second direction and ask her to do both in sequence. She will need to remember to touch her nose and then go on to the second command. Keep adding directions and see how many she can remember in sequence. Children love this game.

- **Cook together.** Find a simple recipe and enjoy time in the kitchen together. Reading the directions aloud and then following them carefully is great practice in building active listening skills.

- **Take a Listening Walk.** Go for a nature walk with the express intention of noticing sounds. Shhh. What do you hear? Where is the sound coming from? What is making that sound? You might even keep a listening log and record the things you hear.

- **Play sound pattern games.** Tap on a drum or clap hands

in a variety of different rhythmic patterns and have your child repeat the sounds. You can play the same game by counting and clapping the syllables in words.
- **Play the old standby, Simon Says.** This game is not only fun for children; it also builds great listening skills. They do not respond unless the leader says, "Simon says."

Family Discussions

You'll do your children a great service if you allow them to enter into family discussions on a regular basis. Make it a habit to pose questions to discuss around the dinner table or in the evenings after dinner. The questions can be simple question and responses at first, such as "What did you enjoy about your day?" or "What is your favorite color and why?" Later you can begin to discuss increasingly challenging topics on a wide variety of topics from social issues to faith questions to political ideology.

When children are encouraged to share their thoughts on a regular basis, they'll gain confidence in both problem-solving and logical thinking. They'll learn the difference between fact and opinion and become better listeners. They'll learn to be kind and respectful of others in these interactions and you'll be surprised at the increase in their speaking vocabularies.

Family Read-alouds

One of the best ways to support reading and have fun doing it is to make time for family read-alouds. Choose a book with plenty of action and enough chapters to keep the family engaged for several days (or more). If the children are fluent readers give them a turn at reading to the rest of the family. Having Mom or Dad read aloud to the whole family is a great way to show that reading is a high value in your home.

Road trips are a great time to do read-alouds or listen to books on tape. You'll find the children will look forward to these times as a highlight of the day. Stories around the campfire, either read alouds or storytelling make for fun times too.

You'll come up with other great ideas for incorporating reading and writing into your family's daily schedules. Your children will reap the benefits in learning and they'll glean a great deal of enjoyment along the way.

Modeling Reading for Information and Pleasure

You can encourage your children to read all day long, but when they see adults reading for the purpose of learning something new or reading as a means of relaxation and fun, they'll actually believe that reading is a valuable use of their time.

Some children naturally love to read. If they're strong readers, they're more motivated to become immersed in the pages. For those who struggle with reading, they'll be much more likely to read if they can pursue books they choose themselves and are motivated to learn about something they love. Even "just average" readers can get pretty excited about books when they find a series or topic that captures their imagination.

Resources

"30,000 Words: Is Your Child Getting Enough?" by Danielle Wood. *Education.com Magazine,* November, 2009

"Talking to Babies Boosts Their Brain Power" by Ian Sample. *The Guardian.com.*

"The Benefits of Talking About Thoughts with Tots" by Rebecca Schwarzlose. *Scientific American,* January, 2014

"The Power of Talking to Your Baby," by Tina Rosenberg. *The*

New York Times, April, 2013

"Listening in Early Childhood " www.listen.org

"Helping Kids with Learning Disabilities Build Listening Skills" by Dr. Kari Miller. *L.A. Special Education Examiner*, March 11, 2011.

Chapter Seven

A Little Drama

The world of drama in all its different forms is a great tool for families who want their children to make their own fun. While we often think of drama taking place in theaters with a cast of tens or more, there are lots and lots of ways to incorporate creative drama games and activities in your own home. And... it's a ton of fun.

Why Drama?

My grandson is a quiet child who loves nothing more than to find a quiet spot alone so he can read. He is kind and gracious to others and quick to forgive. He's sensitive to the point that it's hard not to "protect" him from the real world. But this introverted child got the lead in his small town's production of an off-broadway play. The role required great acting, but in addition dancing and...singing! I was the proudest Grandma around when he belted out the biggest number of the evening like a rock star. Later I asked him how he felt when he did that number. His simple answer was, "Confident." Drama can do wonders for shy children. It can help them break through personal barriers and become brave. I saw it with my own eyes.

The Benefits

Kids love to pretend. Kids love to move their bodies. Voila! Drama incorporates both of these child-friendly activities. Here are some of the benefits of introducing creative drama activities into your family's fun times:

- Creative drama is a great tool for teaching content in other subject areas. Learning about the rainforest? Try some movement games to enhance the understanding of jungle animals. Learning about Shakespeare? Try writing a simple play based on the story of Romeo and Juliet (And act it out).
- Creative drama stimulates creativity and self-expression. It encourages children to get outside their own "selves" and try something new. It gives the opportunity to express a wide range of emotions, thoughts, ideas, that may not be part of everyday life.
- The expression that is the heart of drama builds self-confidence and self-esteem. It goes past nerves and self-consciousness and allows children to try something new with success.
- Learning to act "in character" requires focus, paying attention and engagement—all great learning tools.
- Well-managed drama experiences offer a safe environment to try on other roles and to express feelings. How does it feel and look to be angry? Sad? Afraid?
- Drama experiences build empathy and a chance to support others in their efforts. It is community-building.
- Planning, rehearsing, and then performing offer great feelings of accomplishment and satisfaction.

Theater Games and Activities

Drama teachers often use games and activities to "warm up" their budding actors and actresses. These come in a wide variety of formats, but all of them serve to provide exposure to the art of drama. They may ask children to convey thoughts or feelings, allow them to express an opinion, appeal to one of the five senses, and be done either verbally or nonverbally. The games provide structure within which to explore movement, voice projection, quick thinking and reacting, focus and attention to detail and much more. Here are some of the kinds of drama games that might work in your own home.

- **Mirror Activities**

    Mirror activities are standard drama class fare. They build awareness of body movement and facilitate working together and non-verbal communication. There are many varieties of these games, but the basic game has children working in pairs, facing one another about two-three feet apart. The leader makes a slow, continuous movement and the follower mirror-images the movements. The goal is to succeed, not trick one another. In a more difficult version of this activity there is no leader or follower, the two just act as one. Mirror activities can be done to music as well.

- **Role Plays**

    Role playing games give kids practice in "being" someone else. There are hundreds of ways to begin—scenarios to act out, themes to guide the dialogue, choosing animate or inanimate characters, using verbal or non-verbal responses. Here is an example of a role play game children love.

    Bus Stop is just one example of a role play game. All children available play the game simultaneously. Two people act at a time, the others are guessing their role. Person A sits at the "bus stop"(bench or two chairs) and person B joins him. Each character has secretly chosen an identity. It can be anything—person, animal, machine, etc. Each person speaks in character, trying to guess who or what the other character is. Those waiting for their own turn also guess. Set a specific time for each pair of characters to interact, then ring a bell to end that session. You may choose to divulge the identities or not. When finished, person B moves over and becomes person A with a new identity. A new player joins the game.

Kids love playing this game and it requires almost no props. It's wise to keep a list of possible characters handy for those children who can't think of one quickly.

- **Improvisation**

    In the world of drama, improvisation is a form of live theater in which plot, characters and dialogue of a scene or story are made up in the moment. The entire activity is spontaneous. Often the topic is suggested by an audience member and the actors take it from there. Each performance is unique.

    Improv can be a bit intimidating for those new to it, but improv games can take the fear out of the process through exposure and a "no fail" attitude.

    In improvisation games for kids, the leader selects players, and they draw a topic or scenario from a basket. There is no right or wrong, just responses. Skills will improve with the opportunities to take part in the game. Children will become more and more comfortable with quick responses and actions. Improv is often funny because of the surprising responses.

- **Pantomime**

    Pantomime exercises are non-verbal responses to prompts. They make for great drama guessing games and practice in thinking creatively. If the prompt is office work, the player must think of a way to portray that, possibly by typing on a virtual keyboard or making copies at a virtual copy machine. If the topic is jungle, the actor might act like a monkey.

There are literally hundreds of theater and drama games. Check the resources below to find the right ones for your children.

Puppet Theater

Sock puppets, paper puppets, wooden spoon puppets, paper bag puppets—kids love to make and use puppets to tell their stories. Turn over a table and crouch behind it, or cut out the back of a cardboard box and you have a puppet theater. Write your own script from a favorite fairy tale, folk tale, myth or legend. Or write a script using family members as the characters.

Puppet theater extensions make a great response to a story book that is the current favorite. Children also enjoy writing the exploits of their favorite superhero. The choices are endless as long as you see the opportunity to guide your children toward a hands-on response to something they know, love and are excited about.

Skits

You'll remember skits from summer camp days. Skits are short dramatic responses to some topic or scenario. Write your own or purchase skits from one of the resources below.

Retelling Stories

If you've read my book, Homegrown Readers, you'll know that retelling stories is one of the best ways to increase reading comprehension. The process of remembering the beginning, middle and end of a story, mentioning details about the characters and setting and explaining the resolution of the story are skills that ensure a good understanding of the story content. Oral tradition stories make good retells.

Retells can be done with a bit of flair and become a form of theater. Have your children take turns telling the same story. See who remembers a new bit of information or who can embellish the character. Change the ending of the story. How would that affect the entire story line?

Readers Theater

Reader's Theater, or oral interpretation, is a kind of drama that is low-risk for beginning actors. Children sit on chairs or stools and read a script or story, making their part come to life via great reading and intonation. Reader's theater requires no props or costuming. It's easy and fun and when done over time will encourage strong oral reading skills.

Family Tales

I've mentioned it before, but writing stories based on your own family's activities make for high engagement from the children. Write about the trip to Grandma and Grandpa's house last summer or the hike you took into the mountains. Turn family members into superheroes with superpowers. Take the family on a journey into space...the possibilities are endless and kids think it's great fun to write about and act out the exploits of the family.

Drama in Your Community

Drama is an art form that enriches those involved with it. Be sure to take advantage of local children's theater offerings via schools and theater companies. These theater companies often offer beginning theater classes for children. They're well worth the cost of enrollment. Make drama and dramatic responses part of your family fun.

Resources

Websites with creative drama games and activities
www.childdrama.com
www.creativedrama.orgwww.childdrama.com
www.kidactivities.net
www.bbbpress.com/dramagames
www.slideshare.net
www.home-school.com/ (search drama articles)
www.faceuptheatre.com
www.improv4kids.com/Improvgames
www.theaterfunscripts.com/simpleskits.html
www.creativityinstitute.com/puppettheaterscriptideas.aspx

Books on Creative Drama
The Creative Dramatics Cookbook by Kelley O'Rourke

Learning Through Drama by McGregor, Tate and Robinson

Creative Dramatics in the Classroom and Beyond by Nellie McCaslin

Readers Theatre for Children by Laughlin and Latrobe

Show Time: Music, Dance and Drama Activities for Kids by Lisa Bany-Winters

Seven Steps to Creative Children's Dramatics by Pamela Prince Walker

SECTION
Two

OUTDOOR FAMILY ACTIVITIES

Chapter Eight

OLD-FASHIONED OUTDOOR FUN

Ten Old-Fashioned Outdoor Games to Teach Your Kids

It hardly seems possible, but your children may never have heard of the ten games listed below. They've never spent long spring and summer evenings running around their neighborhoods playing games with the gang. Poor them. Now is the time to teach them the games of your childhood. They'll love them.

Capture the Flag

This old favorite requires a large, flat field such as a soccer field or a park area. Two teams are each trying to capture the other team's flag and return it to their home base. Enemy players can be tagged and put out, sent home, or "frozen" depending on the rules decided upon at the beginning of play. Flags can be a variety of objects from fabric flags to balls. This game requires strategy, leadership and trickery along with running skill and the courage to attack. There are many variations of this game, be sure to choose team leaders and decide on the rules beforehand.

Kick the Can

In this game for a large number of children, a can or similar object is placed in a central location. The person who is "it" counts to a designated number as all the other players hide. "It" tries to defend the can while all the rest of the players attempt to get to the can and kick it before being spotted. Again, there are many variations of this game. Players may be tagged out, or the person who is "it" can simply call out their name as they are spotted.

Duck, Duck, Goose

This circle game for younger children requires no equipment. Children are seated in a circle and one player is "it." The person who is "it" moves around the outer perimeter of the circle, touching each child's head as he says, "duck, duck, duck." At his choosing he touches a head and says "Goose," which is the signal for the seated child to stand and run after the first child. If "goose" can tag the "it" child before running all around the circle to the beginning spot, he is safe, otherwise he becomes the new "it." There are other versions of this same game, for example one in which the toucher is called the fox and the sitters are the hens.

Flashlight Tag

This game is also known as Army Tag or Spotlight. In this tag game players are caught by a flashlight beam. In some versions the "it" person must also accurately call out the name of their captive player. Those caught in the light must either go to a jail spot until they are rescued by another player's tag or they're frozen until released. Only the "it" person has a flashlight. All rescues are done by hand.

Hide and Seek

Also known as Hide and Go Seek, the designated "it" person counts to a number while all other players hide. Players are put out as they're found and the last person to be found is the new "it."

This game originated in 19th century England and traditionally was passed on to younger children by older ones. It has many variations. Some versions have the "it" call out "Olly, olly, oxen free" to signal all players to return to home base.

Mother May I?

One player is Mother (or Father or Captain). All the others line up a distance away facing the Mother. Each player is given instructions in turn. "You may take 5 baby steps" or "You may take two giant steps." The player replies, "Mother, may I?" and the Mother replies, "Yes, you may." If the player forgets to ask permission he or she returns to the starting position. Mother can give backwards steps which also must be obeyed. The player to successfully reach Mother first becomes the leader. A variation of this game is "What's the time, Mr. Fox?" The Fox answers with "It's five o'clock," indicating each player can take five steps. But if he calls out "Dinner Time" or "Midnight" the Fox then chases and tries to catch a player who becomes the Fox.

Statues

Statues is a popular tag game played in many areas of the world. The "it" person turns his or her back on the rest of the players and they are free to move toward a goal until the "it" person turns. When "it" turns, the players must freeze and not be seen moving or they are directed to return to the starting point. Each country has words that the leader must say before turning. Sometimes they count or, for example, in England they may spell out the word London before turning to catch their opponents.

Cat's Cradle

String games have been around for many years. They involve placing string on the fingers and moving in a certain order to create shapes. Some string games have accompanying stories. Cat's Cradle is one popular string game shape. These games have been found all over the world in various cultures. While diagrams are helpful to learn the games, they most often are passed from child to child.

Red Rover

Red Rover is a traditional game first played in England and later played in Australia, Canada and the U.S. Two teams of children face off holding hands, usually about thirty feet apart. The captain of one team calls out, "Red Rover, Red Rover, send ___ right over." That person from the opposing team then runs and tries to break through the hands of two players. If they are successful they are allowed to choose a person to take back to their team. If they fail they become part of the opposing team.

Sardines

In this version of hide and seek one person is it and is allowed to find a hiding place. All the others search for "it" and when they find him or her they join in hiding in that spot. (Thus beginning to feel like sardines) Each player in turn joins the hiding spot until one last person becomes the new "it."

The rules to all of these games are simple and a minimum of equipment is needed. There is a lot of running and physical exercise. The joy is in the play. Share these old-fashioned games with your children—soon.

For more retroactive outdoor games see ***RetroActive Skip, Hop and You Don't Stop*** by Tom O'Leary. This book contains directions and rules for over one hundred childhood games.

International Games

Down, Down from Australia

This is a game of catch with a lightweight ball such as a

tennis ball. Children toss the ball until someone misses and then they chant, "Down on one knee." Play progresses with that child continuing play in the assigned position. A second miss brings the call, "Down on Two Knees. Successive misses are Down on one elbow, then two, and finally Down on Your Chin. This usually brings the game to closure and a new game begins.

What's the Time, Mr. Wolf from Italy

This game is related to Red Light, Green Light. One child is Mr. Wolf and stands with his back to the group. When the children call out, What's the time, Mr. Wolf?" the wolf responds with a time such as "It's ten o'clock." This entitles each child to take ten steps closer to Mr. Wolf. When the children are very close, and the question is asked, Mr. Wolf responds by saying, It's time for dinner!" and chasing the children with the goal of catching one to become the new Mr. Wolf.

Up and Down (Oonch, Neech) from Pakistan

This is a traditional game of tag with the exception being that safe zones are anywhere you can climb to—chairs, tree branches, porches, etc. Children run from the one who is it, but are safe if they can make it to the safe zones.

Pilolo from Ghana

Pilolo means "Time to search." The game requires a timekeeper and a leader. The timekeeper stands at the end point. The leader hides an object such as a stick or a certain stone while the players hide their eyes. The object may be hidden anywhere—in trees, in sand, or any good hiding place. The leader announces "Pilolo" and the timekeeper starts the stopwatch or marks time on a clock. Children search for the hidden object and when they find it they run to the finish line. The game may be played for a certain amount of time and the timekeeper keeps score. Children who find the object successfully and run to the end spot are in contention for winning the game with the lowest number of minutes and seconds.

Intergenerational Fun:
Ten Activities to Do When the Whole Family Gathers

Once in a while you may be fortunate enough to gather the extended family clan. Maybe it's centered around a wedding or other family event such as a reunion. Maybe it's as simple as the grandparents annual visit. How can you keep everyone entertained and happy from Grandpa to the youngest grandchild? Of course you'll plan great meals and some outings, but what can you do on long afternoons or evenings when there are family members of all ages to include?

Here are some fun ideas to keep the "children of all ages" happy. You might even want to create teams in which there are individuals from each generation represented and working together to have a great time.

1. **Plan a family nature walk and scavenger hunt.** Choose an area where the pathways are either paved or relatively flat for the older members of the crew. Have a list of items to give to each family team. Allow a set amount of time to wander and collect and a time when each team has to report back to the beginning site. Be sure to make some of the items you're searching for easy to find and some that are more challenging. When all the teams have reported in, give out small prizes for the winners and maybe even include a booby prize for the last place. Make the event lighthearted fun and enjoy your walk at the same time.

2. **Make rock garden mementos** to take home with you. Find some nice, flat rocks. Wash and dry them. Then apply one coat of decoupage glue. Decorate with stickers, leaves or flower petals; add beautiful words with a permanent

marker such as "joy", "family", or maybe the surname of the family members. Then add a second coat of glue and allow your rocks to dry. Take them home and place them in the garden or on the patio as a way of remembering your fun times together. The grandkids will love this one.

3. Create a **family bingo game** from photocopied pictures of all the family members. Place pictures on pieces of cardboard in a bingo pattern of five rows with a free space in the middle. Also create call cards to match. Use some buttons, squares of paper or other objects as markers and then begin playing. Everyone will laugh when they hear, B—Grandma Allen or G—Baby Ethan. Have small prizes for winners.

4. **Build an outdoor fort** and use it as a gathering place for meals and other fun times. This is a great activity for the children in the group. Designate blankets, tarps, rope, chairs and any other items needed to create a comfortable space in which to spend great family time.

5. Play a **Family Trivia game.** Choose a family member who is rich in family lore to write lots of family questions and matching answers. Bring them along to the gathering and then split into two teams. The creator of the game can be the game host and the team with the most correct answers wins. Plan on plenty of laughter when you ask a question like, "How many hot dogs did Uncle Bernie eat at the last 4th of July barbecue?" Or which family ancestor came out west on a covered wagon?"

6. Do a **Frame It craft** with all sorts of found items. If you're near a beach gather shells, bits of driftwood and beach glass. If you're near a forest, pick up beautiful leaves and twigs. Whatever you find, manipulate the pieces into a larger shape such as a fish or the family surname initial. Paint a piece of cardboard with glue and secure the items, then place them in a standard picture frame to take

home and admire. An 8" X 10" frame works well for this project and younger grandkids can team up with an older member of the family.

7. Find a driveway, or other paved area in which to conduct **your family chalk art gallery**. Select smaller teams of three or four and then allow a set amount of time in which to create a team masterpiece. You might provide a theme for the event such as "the things we love" or "our favorite pastimes." Have a family member act as judge and award small prizes, with every team winning some award such as "best in show" or "most creative."

8. Bring along supplies to help every family member **create their own rhythm or musical instrument.** You'll find lots of ideas at Activity Village. All you need is some sort of container and something inside to make a noise. Spend the afternoon creating the instruments and then allow practice time. Enjoy a concert at evening time. Maybe you'll want to schedule the concert outdoors in the family fort. You might want to play some background music or encourage presenters to sing a song while they use their drums, shakers and kazoos.

9. Do some sort of **craft** such as making paper flowers, creating a greeting card or designing some sort of paper weight. Make the craft with others in mind. Then on your way home **deliver your gifts to a local nursing home or an assisted living**. Give the family the pleasure of giving to others.

10. Plan an **evening Star Watch**. Bring along some books on the constellations and stars. Take some time to share information and then when it's nice and dark outside, take the whole clan out to star watch. If someone owns a telescope, all the better. Identify constellations and note how they move over time. This "happening" will be one to remember.

One of the best gifts you can give your family are the memories you'll create when you have fun together. Both grandparents and grandkids and everyone in between will have a time to remember.

Unstructured Outdoor Play:
A Plea for More Time Out of Doors

My brother and I spent countless hours playing outdoors. We built forts and hideouts. We imagined we were digging to China and we made mud pies. We caught grasshoppers in jars and rolled down grassy hills. We used found objects like ferns, grasses and stones to become part of our outdoor creations. We made up our own games and sometimes just sat on the ground and enjoyed the sights and smells around us. Lucky for us, this type of unstructured outdoor play was then the norm.

Children today don't have the opportunity to play out of doors much unless it is in a structured team sport or an organized "run." Team sports are great for a number of reasons, but they aren't the same as unstructured, open-ended creative play.

Many voices in the world of Education and Child Psychology warn us we're in danger of losing a very important aspect of child development related to child-powered creative play. You, the parent, can be the catalyst for building plenty of outdoor time into your child's schedule with no specific product or result expected other than pure enjoyment.

Here are some resources to inform and encourage you to support more outdoor exploration in your child's schedule:

How to Raise a Wild Child: The Art and Science of Falling in Love with Nature by Scott D. Sampson

I Love Dirt! 52 Activities to Help You and Your Kids Discover the Wonders of Nature by Jennifer Ward

Balanced and Barefoot: How unrestricted Outdoor Play Makes for Strong, Confident, and Capable Children by Angela Hanscomb

Beyond Remote-Controlled Childhood by Diane E. Levin

The Nature Connection: An Outdoor Workbook for Kids, Families and Classrooms by Clare Walker Leslie.

Last Child in the Woods: Saving Our Children from Nature-deficit Disorder by Richard Louv

Chapter Nine

Get Your Hands Dirty

Nothing is quite as satisfying as planting a seed and watching it grow into a plant over time. As if by magic the germination takes place underground, out of sight, but eventually a seedling peeks through the soil.

Children love to plant things and watch them grow. Whether it's vegetable seeds or flower seeds, the pay-off when the sprout appears never fails to please. And there is a lot to learn from gardening. Children learn practical information about where our food supplies originate, the life cycle of plants, the care and feeding of healthy plants and the wonder of the variety of plants found in nature.

It's fun to start small with young children. Allow them to plant seeds in small beds or in containers. Help them remember to care for the plant as it germinates and grows. You might keep charts on the growth of the plant over time, or draw pictures of each stage of growth.

Later children can take on the real jobs of planting, weeding, watering and otherwise caring for the garden. They can help with the harvest and preservation of foods or enjoy the process of gathering, washing and eating fresh produce directly from the garden.

There are any number of fun mini-gardening projects to whet your child's appetite for getting his or her hands dirty. Here are some of the best:

Sunflower Houses

Sunflowers are magnificent things to plant because they have a short germination time, as little as seven days, and they grow spectacularly tall. Children will love planting their sunflower home and then watching it grow inch by inch over the coming months. You could even do a little mapping and graphing as the home is planned. And then, when the magic is done, the kids can play in the house all day and sleep out in their sleeping bags at night.

www.greeneducationfoundation.org How to Build a Sunflower House

Gourds on a Fence

Planting a row of gourds along a fenceline is a great way to enjoy the growth of these beautiful and varied plants. Kids love their beautiful colors and shapes. Gourds need to grow and mature until all the greenery has dried up. Then, when the gourds are thoroughly dry, you can use them for decoration, for rhythm instruments, or hollow them out to make homegrown birdhouses.

www.foothillsfarm.com Ginny's Gourds

Pumpkins to Jack-o-Lanterns

Pumpkin seeds are easy to plant in mounds of soil with seeds spaced four to five inches apart. They'll grow all summer long and bloom with their trademark orange blossoms. Then in the fall they turn from green globes to nice, fat, orange pumpkins. Use them for cooking pies and tarts, but be sure to set aside several to

hollow out and carve into Halloween jack-o-lanterns.
www.allaboutpumpkins.com

Succulents in Clam Shells

Succulents are those interesting plants that retain water in their fat leaves and come in all shapes and sizes. They are the hens and chicks, the sedums and the sempervivums that look like green roses. These plants, especially when grouped together make truly lovely arrangements. The fun part is they can grow in a minimum of soil and are perfect for a kid project. Take a large shell (or other interesting container), and drill several small holes in the bottom for drainage. Then place a layer of wet sphagnum moss in the bottom. Top with potting soil and then add several succulent plants close together. These make nice gifts or just place them in a spot where you and your children can enjoy them throughout the year.
www.simplysucculents.com
And a few more...

Food Scrap Gardens

Be intentional about this one. Gather orange, lemon or lime seeds and plant them in potting soil. Or save an avocado or mango seed and then plant in water until it sprouts. Ginger root is also easy to root and create a new plant. Garlic cloves or onion bulbs grow new plants in short order too.

These projects are great for introductory lessons on the growing cycle of plants and take a minimum of space in your sunny windows.

Grow Your Own Salad

Plant a variety of greens in containers and put them in a sunny window. The seeds will sprout quickly and you can enjoy lettuces, spinach, kale and other healthy greens all year round.

Plant a Pizza Garden

What fun. You can help your children plant a garden that will eventually turn into their own homemade pizza. Plant tomatoes, basil, oregano, peppers and onion in the shape of a pizza with each triangle "piece" a different plant.

Make a Bean Tepee

Tie three stakes together and plant pole beans beneath them. Beans sprout and climb quickly and your kids will love the anticipation of growing a fun place in which to hide and play.

Three Sisters

Native Americans have grown these three healthy plants together for hundreds of years. Plant corn, beans and squash in the same area. The corn will grow tall, the beans to a medium bushy height and the squash will cover the ground. All three make healthy eating.

Plant a Butterfly Garden

Attract beautiful butterflies to your yard by putting in plants with brilliant blooms. Daisies, zinnias, red clover, phlox, milkweed and the lovely purple-bloomed butterfly bush will bring the butterflies to you.

Portable Flower Garden

Plant a mini flower garden in an old wagon or wheelbarrow. The plants will sprout quickly in the shallow warmth and you can even move the garden to maximize sunshine.

You can spark your family's interest in the great out of doors with these and similar gardening projects. For more fun projects to do together see www.kidsgardening.org.

Great Introductory Gardening Books for Young Children

Here is a list of ten wonderful gardening books for children. As you read them together you'll introduce kids to the beauty of the plant world and also to the joys of getting their hands dirty in their very own garden.

Fiction

The Carrot Seed by Ruth Krauss and Crockett Johnson

This classic is now available in its 60th edition. A young boy plants a carrot seed. Everyone tells him it won't grow, but he believes it will. He waters, weeds and waits. Children love the anticipation created by the simple words and pictures. First published in 1945, this story remains a childhood favorite.

Planting a Rainbow by Lois Ehlert

This book teaches children how to plant bulbs, seeds and seedlings and how to nurture their growth. Bright and beautiful collage illustrations picture all the flowers of each color of the rainbow. This book is a visual treat for parents and kids alike. Little fingers will itch to begin planting.

City Green by DyAnne DiSalvo-Ryan

Gardens can be grown in the middle of a bustling city neighborhood—just ask Marcy and her friend Miss Rosa. Kids will champion Marcy's gardening efforts as an entire community gets in on the project. Pencil and watercolor illustrations add beauty to this endearing story. The book includes a real-life page of instructions for starting your own neighborhood's community garden.

Growing Vegetable Soup by Lois Ehlert

Bright primary colors are the hallmark of this beautiful book, *Growing Vegetable Soup*. No soup from a can here, as children are introduced to the tools necessary for growing a garden and clear pictures of each seed and the plant that grows from it. The best part of all is the eventual harvest and the fun of creating your family's very own vegetable soup grown in your own garden space. The recipe is included.

Sunflower House by Eve Bunting

Watercolors and colored pencil drawings grace this story. A young boy grows his own outdoor house with sunflower seeds. He plants them in a circle, tends them and then enjoys long summer days and nights in his sunny home. When the seeds are ripe he shares some with the birds and keeps the rest for next year's secret summer hideout.

Non-fiction

Roots, Shoots, Buckets and Boots by Sharon Lovejoy

Lovejoy is a nationally known gardener with her own television specials and gardening projects done in her California home. She has introduced thousands of children to the fun of gardening. In this book she encourages a love of gardening by sharing such creative gardening projects as planting a pizza garden and growing the "three sisters of life" like the native Iriquois Indians. Children can enjoy a harvest celebration by making Indian corn jewelry and cornstalk animals. Tutored by her own botanist grandmother, Lovejoy's enthusiasm for gardening jumps right off the pages.

The Children's Kitchen Garden by Georgeanne and Ethel Brennan

Based on a gardening project done at the French-American School in Berkeley, California, this book teaches children first-hand the connection between gardening and the food we eat.

The recipes are mostly vegetarian and include Corn, Rice and Tomato Salad with Basil, and Snapbean and Potato Soup. *The Children's Kitchen Garden* is great for first-time gardeners and offers a resource section for ordering seeds.

Gardening Wizardry for Kids: Green Thumb Magic for the Great Indoors by L. Patricia Kite and Yvette Santiago Banek

Why not engage your children in a little gardening science? This book has over 300 experiments with projects for everything from a windowsill to a gigantic outdoor garden. It begins with a history of various plants. The book is useful to both parents and teachers as its scientific approach to growing plants asks questions such as "Do radish seedlings always grow toward the light?" and "How does water get from carrot roots into stems?"

Grow Your Own Pizza: Gardening Plans and Recipes for Kids by Constance Hardesty

Kids Gardening 101 here. The fundamentals of gardening from composting and mulching to harvesting the crop are outlined for older readers. Garden maintenance, dealing with pests and safety tips are taught by Hardesty who is an instructor at the Denver Botanic Gardens in Colorado. Hardesty conducts children's garden tours and has worked as a children's cook, creating fun kids meals with fresh veggies.

Bonus Book

Finally, you must try the classic I Can Read book by Millicent Selsam entitled *Seeds and More Seeds*. In this easy-to-read classic, young Benny begins to wonder about seeds. What are they, how do they grow and what will they turn into? Read this simple book to your child, or better yet, allow him or her to read it to you, and then watch as enthusiasm for getting out into nature grows into a passion for planting and watching things grow!

Chapter Ten

Outdoor Family Outings

Nature Walks, Field Guides and Kid Collections

When my middle grandson was four and five he was absolutely crazy about birds. He wanted to check out every bird book and bird field guide available. He drew birds and studied their habitats, he learned to identify all the birds that live in his area. If he'd been a famous artist, this certainly would have been his "bird period."

Your children can learn to love nature. Given just the smallest nudge in the direction of nature walks, children will learn to appreciate the out of doors. They can practice getting quiet and observing. What do they hear? What do they see and smell? I used to tell my own children to "go outside and find something beautiful." And they did. Then they brought it to me to appreciate. You can help to develop this wonder at the beauty and intricacies of nature in your own children.

One of the most exciting roles we play as parents is opening doors to learning whenever possible. All around us are amazing creations—birds, animals, trees and flowers. Children will respond to learning about the natural flora and fauna of your neighborhood and other places you visit if you introduce them to the information.

One of the best ways to introduce information on the natural world is through **field guides.** Children love the format of field guides with their abundance of information in a variety of charts, graphs, labels and pictures. Here are two websites that list excellent field guides:

Nature Watch: offers a huge variety of field guides for children. Choose from Arctic Wildlife, bugs, birds, butterflies, wildflowers, beetles and much more. (www.nature-watch.com)

Acorn Naturalists: has field guides for constellations, rocks and minerals, trees, insects, birds, reptiles and amphibians. (www.acornnaturalists.com)

Kid Collections:
A Great Way to Boost Science Processing Skills

Another way to encourage a love of the out of doors is through collections. Have you noticed that any time you're outside with children they naturally begin to pick things up and "collect" them? It's part of their natural curiosity about the world and it's a wonderful thing. Nurture that curiosity by encouraging your children to make collections of all kinds. Younger children can choose three or four treasures to save and display. Older children are able to do ever more detailed collections of all kinds.

In addition to awakening the wonder at the vast bounty of our natural world, children also respond to the "fun of the hunt" involved in collecting things. From an educational point of view, collections also lend themselves to basic math and science learning. Younger children can sort by size, color, shape and pattern. Older children will learn to identify, label, organize into categories and classify their treasures in many different ways. Parents can support these learning activities by allowing collections display space in the home. Many children enjoy creating their own "museum" for a period of time. They will naturally want to add drawings, short informational descriptions, and charts. Voila! You have created an engaged learner!

What to collect? The possibilities are endless. Some favorites from the natural world include rocks and minerals, shells, feathers, bark, leaves, pinecones, insects, butterflies and moths. Other collectibles might include coins, stamps, stickers, miniature toys, dolls, bottle caps, comic books, gum wrappers, buttons or marbles. If there are a lot of them around, you can collect them.

Support your children's wonder and joy in the intricacies of nature by creating lists of beautiful things seen, favorite hikes or places to play and anything else that builds children's appreciation of the beauty around us. Display the charts and lists on walls to be read and enjoyed in times to come. Such activities will increase logical thinking skills and will involve organization of factual information in the process of writing.

Children who develop a passion for their collections will also gain self-confidence and will learn to share their passion with others. They'll talk about their collections, share and trade items with others, and otherwise engage in social skills. They will "own" their collection in such a way as to gain in responsibility and care-giving of something valuable to them.

They'll increase their knowledge base of a certain subject area. If they have chosen to collect bird nests they may also learn all about the habitats of birds, their diet, their size, shape and defining marks. They'll want to observe birds in their natural habitat and they'll ask questions, make inferences, synthesize information and engage in many scientific processing skills. They will be independent learners.

Adults can further encourage such independent learning by purchasing appropriate books, field guides and posters related to the collection of the day. You might even want to have a disposable camera or binoculars on hand for capturing images during impromptu nature walks. Keep poster board on hand to be ready for those inspired lists, charts and drawings that will make up displays of collected items. See the following list of ideas to get you started. Happy collecting!

Books on Kid Collections

The Kids' Nature Book: 365 Indoor/Outdoor Activities and Experiences by Susan Milford

Nature Smart: A Family Guide to Nature by Tekiela and Shanber

Field Guides by theAudubon Society

The Insect Book: A Basic Guide to Collection and Care of Common Insects for Young Children, by Connie Zakowski

Kids Collect: Amazing Collections for Fun, Crafts and Science Fair Projects by Dan and Mary Hubley

Collecting Bugs and Things by Julia Spencer

Collecting Things is Fun by Kimberlee Graves

The Usborne Book of Collecting Things by Ray Gibson

Let's Go Rock Collecting by Roma Gans and Holly Keller

Craft items to keep on hand for displaying collections:

- Cardboard boxes and the inside dividers
- Tape
- Glue
- Markers
- String, twine
- Scissors
- Fabric scraps
- Clothespins to hand items
- Lumber scraps
- Styrofoam trays
- Cans
- Plastic containers with lids
- Old picture frames
- Saran Wrap

- Clear contact paper
- Paper bags
- Plastic bags
- Clip Boards for recording data
- Children's binoculars
- Waxed paper

Boost Your Child's Science Skills

You may not realize it but when encouraging your children to make displays of collected items, you're paving the way for your child's future science lessons. Your kids will be learning and using the following basic science processing skills:

Observation: Noticing alike and different, noticing unique features, using our five senses to record information.

Classification: Sorting and Organizing according to a property such as size, shape or color.

Measurement: Finding the length, width, or other quantity using a measuring tool.

Communication: Sharing information with others, relating facts.

Making inferences: Using data to speculate on factual information.

Making predictions: Using data to predict an outcome.

Interpretation of factual data: Making meaning from data gathered, answering questions posed.

Experimentation: Posing questions, designing a test, logging data and trying out possible solutions to problems.

Inquiry: Asking appropriate questions to determine an outcome or evaluate a circumstance.

It's easy to see that once a kid collection is created and displayed it sets the stage for further learning in both science and math. How long is each pinecone? How many different kinds of rocks are found in the back yard? Which leaf has the most veins in it?

They're also great for teaching children to ask their own questions. "I wonder if bigger pinecones contain more seeds than smaller ones? Are there more green or yellow leaves? Could it be that perching birds have different feet than water birds?

Camp Outs

If your family has a long history of camping and is totally outdoor-savvy then you need read no further. But if your children haven't been camping before and you'd like to take them, there are some important points to take into consideration.

Much as we would like it to be otherwise, many of our children have become indoor creatures. They don't play outside unless they're playing an organized sport. It seems that old-fashioned playing is a bit of a dinosaur these days. There are some good reasons for this, one of them being safety. It's no longer safe for children to play unsupervised in their neighborhoods. Also the indoor trend is the result of technology. All of our computers, video games and other screened entertainments occupy children without challenging them to physical activity.

So there we are, with children unused to the outdoors. That said, there are so many good reasons to get out into nature; learning about the flora and fauna of an area, relaxing in the company of family and friends and building healthier bodies and minds. It's a great thing to do.

As you begin to think about a camping trip you'll want to ask:

1) **Where?**

    A first-time venture probably should be relatively close

to home and shouldn't be overly challenging in terms of comfort and endurance. Perhaps it would be best to choose a place with bathrooms and showers and maybe even a children's play area. After all you want the children to have a good time and a Spartan trip, especially if the weather doesn't cooperate, will only ensure that it's the last trip for your children. When you've found a suitable place, be sure to include some bona fide camping experiences such as day hikes, fishing, boating and the traditional evening campfire.

2) **When?**

Reservations usually have to be made at campgrounds a year ahead of time. Often in addition to the nightly fees, you'll have to pay an additional campground entrance fee. Be sure to arrive at the campground area as early in the day as possible. It's no fun trying to set up camp in the dark!

3) **What to do?**

Taking some time to plan for this first camping adventure will pay dividends. First of all plan activities for the drive. A small game to play in the car or games such as "find the license plate" will keep children occupied during the drive and avoid the "Are we there yet?" Plan quick and easy meals and include disposable plates and cups, etc. If you really want to be more "green," then make the cooking and clean-up including washing up dishes part of the fun. Perhaps there could be partners, one adult and one child responsible for each meal. Remember how much fun the evening campfires can be with songs, stories, and special treats like s'mores. Some of the larger campgrounds have park rangers who will lead daytime activities or have evening slideshows and talks. Be prepared if the weather turns bad. Simple raingear can be a lifesaver as well as games and activities to do inside the tent if necessary.

4) **Enjoy**

When you've done all your planning, be sure to take along plenty of enthusiasm. Children will pick up on the fun if you are eager and ready to have fun too. Be creative—maybe you'll see some wildlife, or catch a trout or spot a certain bird or butterfly. Once again knowing your children's current hobbies and interests may help you to plan things they will be sure to enjoy. This is also a great time to share your areas of expertise. Do you know all about wildflowers or can you teach the children how to paddle a canoe?

Now you're all set. Be sure to take along a camera to document all the fun. Kids are certain to enjoy the camping event **and** all the stories and memories of their first camping experience.

Quick and Easy Meals for Campers

English Muffin Pizzas: Use English muffins, squeezable pizza sauce and shredded mozzarella. Toast muffin halves on oiled grill. Turn over and spread with sauce, cheese and any toppings your family enjoys. Serve when the cheese melts.

Grilled PBJ: This one is a cinch. Choose a hearty bread and be generous with the fillings. Butter on both sides and toast on your grill. They'll stick to your ribs.

Coffee Can Stew: Cut stew meat into small pieces. Place meat in a clean coffee can with 2T. butter. Brown meat over the fire. Add red potatoes, baby carrots and onions with 2T. more butter. Cover with foil and place in the fire for 20 minutes.

Banana Boats: Slit unpeeled bananas lengthwise without cutting through. Fill the opening with mini-marshmallows and chocolate chips. Sprinkle with brown sugar, wrap in foil and place either on a grill or in the coals of your fire. They're ready in just seven minutes.

Eggs in a Hat: You may want a change from morning cereal or pancakes. Try this fun recipe. Grease a hot griddle. Cut a hole in pieces of bread using a cup or glass. Toast the bread on both sides and crack an egg in the hole. When the egg is solid, flip the bread. Top with a slice of your favorite cheese and a slice of ham. Serve when cheese is nicely melted.

Local History Tours

Another way to enjoy the out of doors and include beneficial learning experiences, is to take advantage of the historical landmarks in your area or wherever you may visit. Such outings may take you to forts or museums, natural landscapes such as mountains, rivers, waterfalls, and the like. Or you may find yourselves on a quest to track the lives of famous people and search through historical libraries or pioneer cemeteries.

Many of our states boast historical ties to famous Americans such as Lewis and Clark, various war heroes, Presidents and literary figures. Homes of famous people are often open for tours, century home and working heritage farms are another source of history up close and personal.

Do a little research on the part of the country you call home. What can your family study and learn together?

Benefits of Studying Local History

While we often think of history as a long string of boring facts and places, there are many good reasons to learn about our past. Children will gain a sense of societies and cultures, they'll become aware of innovations and inventions that have changed the way people live and they'll identify important characters from the past. They'll learn lessons on human behavior over time and gain a sense of identity as they learn about "their people."

In addition, when children learn about real-life history they gain skills in critical thinking such as assessing evidence to support a point, dealing with conflicting interpretations of past affairs and they move toward becoming informed citizens of their country and world.

Get to know your part of the world. Introduce your children to the plants, animals, and the natural wonders around you. Learn about the history. Get out into the great out of doors and teach your children to love and appreciate it.

Chapter Eleven

Treasure Hunts

When I was in second or third grade there was a story in my reading book that captured my imagination in a big way. It was Dick, Jane and the neighborhood gang, along with Spot, having fun following clues. The clues took them all over the neighborhood with the final one leading to a fantastic prize. (A prize which has escaped my memory.) That story made me shivery-excited.

Never underestimate the power of a treasure hunt in the minds and hearts of young children. What seems simple and mundane to us, can fill their hearts with thrilling experiences of adventure and mystery.

The best part for parents, is the ease of preparing a treasure hunt or scavenger hunt to delight your littles. There are wonderful ideas for planning these satisfying activities in the resources listed below.

Treasure Hunts vs. Scavenger Hunts

Both of these activities are great fun for kids, but are slightly different from one another. A **treasure hunt** is a search leading to a prize. Players follow clues, often in the form of riddles, to move from one place to another in the quest for finding the final treasure.

A **scavenger hunt** begins with a list of objects to find and often comes with a time limit. Players may find all or part of the list, may have to draw, take pictures, or otherwise prove their finds, and may work in teams. Those finding the most items on the list, wins.

Themed treasure hunts and scavenger hunts are popular and come in a wide variety of topics. They are perfect activities for parties and lend themselves to family gatherings, picnics, camping outings and the like. They're also wonderful for a long, lazy afternoon when children need something new and different to pep up the day. Treasure hunts and scavenger hunts may be done indoors or out, depending on the items to be found.

Planning a Treasure Hunt

When planning a treasure hunt, keep the following in mind:

- **Your audience**. Take into account the age level, reading ability, physical abilities, and so forth as you write your clues. If there is a wide range in the ages of players, consider having the participants work in teams.
- **Group Size**. Are you playing with six kids or twenty? What is the range of the playing area?
- **Clues**. Write clues or riddles at the appropriate difficulty level.
- **Decide on your rules.** Be clear on boundaries to stay within, time period in which to play, how to "prove" you found the items in a scavenger hunt, and safety or respect for property issues.

Choose from a list of themes such as:

- Nature

Homegrown Family Fun ~ Unplugged

- Beach
- Forest
- Camping
- Knowledge of a certain field of study
- Circus
- Road Trip
- Animals
- The library or museum
- The dictionary
- People-watching

Following are resources to search for the perfect treasure or scavenger hunt for your family. You'll find that printable materials are available in many subjects and topics.

Websites

www.handsonaswegrow.com
www.buggyandbuddy.com/scavenger-hunt-kids
www.mudkidsadventures.com
www.scaventer-hunt-fun.com
www.scavengerhuntclues.org
www.scavenger-hunt-guru.com

Books

Ultimate Treasure Hunt Guide by Lisa Mason

Magic Kingdom Photo Scavenger Hunts by Emma Stewart

Treasure and Scavenger Hunts: How to Plan, Create and Give Them by Gordon Burgett

Treasure and Scavenger Hunts by Gordon Burgett

Travel Scavenger Hunt Card Game from University Games

100 Ready-to-Use Treasure Hunt Clues by Gordon Burgett

Jan Pierce, M.Ed.

Scavenger Hunts for Kids by Christy Davis

Treasure Hunts for Kids by Christy Davis

How to Make Your Own Simple Treasure Hunts by Sam Gething-Lewis

Fun with Scavenger Hunts by M.J. Kusz

Letterboxing: The Ultimate Family Treasure Hunt

If your children love a scavenger hunt, following clues and looking for "treasure," they'll love letterboxing. Letterboxing, an outdoor activity that can be done all across the United States, combines the fun of the hunt with beginning orienteering skills. Die-hard Letterboxers hide small weatherproof containers in public places such as parks and along hiking trails. They post clues to the whereabouts of these boxes on the internet. Once found, the boxes contain a log book and a rubber stamp. Finders sign the book, usually adding their own unique stamp, and then impress the stamp from the box in their own personal log book.

Letterboxing began in England in 1854 when a National Park guide named James Perrott left a bottle by Cranmere Pool with his calling card inside. He then invited others to add their own cards. Later visitors began to leave postcards or notes hoping the next visitors would return them by mail, thus the name Letterboxing. The letterboxing fun began in the U.S. in 1998 after the Smithsonian magazine published an article about it. There are over 20,000 letterboxes hidden in the U.S. today. Some people hiding boxes give out clues by word of mouth only, making the hunt even more challenging.

I've done letterboxing with my three grandsons for the past four years. We select a nearby park or a small town by the beach or perhaps a destination such as last year's Tillamook Forestry Center on Oregon's Highway 16. We found two letterboxing sites on the grounds of the Forestry Center and learned that the volunteers who run the beautiful and informational mini-museum had no idea they were there. Our family letterboxing days are perfect outings for all ages. Grandpa enjoys getting out and about with the children, Grandma enjoys seeing the gleam in the boys' eyes as they gear up for the hunt, the oldest boy enjoys reading the clues for all of us and then we get into "Raccoon Mode," the name of our letterboxing team. We've had great success following the clues and finding the boxes. We have nearly as much fun adding our names, The Raccoons, to the ledger in each box and replacing it carefully, being quite sure no one sees us as we put the box back in place for the next letterboxing team.

Letterboxing with your children is the perfect family day out of doors. Be sure to pack snacks and perhaps a picnic lunch as you "hit the trails." To begin letterboxing you need to gather a pencil or pen, a small sketch book, one or more ink pads and a stamp, a simple compass and your clues (found online). You'll build excitement for the hunt as you search online for likely boxes to find. Sometimes the boxes are placed in a series based on a theme such as pirates or animals, and other times there is only one box to find. Some clues include simple compass reading and all of them involve careful reading, thinking and direction following. You'll have the opportunity to teach basic environmental rules such as leaving the box carefully restored to its hiding place and leaving a site in better condition than you found it. And, no group of hunters is ready to go until they choose a trail name to identify themselves in the log book. You can be The Squirrels or The Wild Johnson Clan.

If you become expert letterbox finders you may want to jump up to the next level of participation—the ones who create and hide boxes. Creating letterboxes requires familiarity with an outdoor setting, writing clear but slightly tricky clues and then hiding the boxes in secure places. Once that is done, you'll need to post the clues online. Often those creating the boxes carve their own stamps to go with their theme. Creators of boxes should check on them periodically to make sure they're still safe and ready to find. The online sites will tell if some boxes are "retired." You'll need to prepare yourselves for not finding the boxes every time as some are lost or just very difficult to find—that's part of the challenge. So make a plan with your favorite treasure hunters and begin the adventures soon. It's easy to get on letterboxing websites to look for an outdoor site you already enjoy. Chances are someone has chosen it as a place to hide letterboxes. Happy Hunting!

To get started go to: http://www.letterboxing.org/. You'll find everything you need to know to begin your letterboxing adventures. Be sure to visit the children's page and see pictures of happy Letterboxers.

Letterboxing Supply List

- Clues found online. They will direct you to the "treasure."
- A notebook in which to collect stamps found in letterboxes.
- Pens and pencils to sign your team name in the logbook.
- A stamp and stamp pads. The stamp can be homemade to reflect your team name.

  You'll add your stamp to the notebook in the hidden box.
- A compass.
- Snacks and a picnic lunch.
- A camera to record your fun.

Another Family Treasure Hunt: Geocaching

Geocaching is a higher-level treasure hunt activity that requires a GPS receiver plus a set of coordinates and sometimes a list of clues. The search is on for a cache of goodies in an eco-friendly site.

A cache is a hidden container with a logbook, pencil or pen, some trinkets and possibly a disposable camera. It's all placed in a weatherproof box and hidden in a natural setting. The key to finding the caches is in following the GPS coordinates, posted on various websites. The most popular of these sites is www.geocaching.com. Caches often use a five star system to rate the level of difficulty and the terrain.

Basic rules for geocaching include:
- Caches must not be placed on private land without permission or in national parks or wilderness areas ever.
- Do not cross private land without permission to reach a geocache site.
- Do not include offensive materials in a cache.
- Leave no trace of your presence after finding and replacing the cache.
- You may add trinkets to the cache.
- Some coordinates require solving riddles, codes or ciphers.
- Some clues are encrypted.
- Some caches used to be virtual, but this is no longer allowed. Virtual cache hunting is a relatively new hobby known as "waymarking."

Geocaching is free of charge and comes with the benefit of building skills in map reading and geography while problem-solving and enjoying an outing in a natural setting.

Practical Rules for Geocaching:
- The geocache must be placed so it's unnoticeable to passers-by yet accessible without harming the terrain or vegetation.
- The cache should be camouflaged by surrounding natural features.
- A geocacher must never reveal the location of the hiding

spot to others.
- You should sign the register found inside the cache to let the owner know you found it.
- Exchange trinkets of equal or greater value than what you take.
- Travel bugs are different than trinkets. They are meant to travel the world. You may take it if you promise to place it in another cache. Log the travel bug number when you replace it so the owner can track its travel.
- When done with a geocache, replace it exactly where you found it.
- A time-honored tradition in geocaching is to "cache in, trash out" which means you leave the cache area as clean or even better than when you found it.

A GPS will get you to within ten to twenty feet of the cache. After that the hunter must use problem-solving skills to determine a natural hiding place in that area.

Though some detractors call geocaching a "hobby that requires thousands of dollars in military hardware to search out Tupperware containers," the hobby is here to stay. Remember that a GPS is a radio receiver that requires a clear view of the sky for best reception. Learn to use the compass view which tells you the bearing and distance to your intended cache.

Geocaching, an advanced form of treasure hunting, can be a wonderful addition to your next family road trip.

Resources

Books

Local Treasures: Geocaching Across America by Margot Anne Kelley

Geocaching: 64 Success Secrets by Marie Barrerra

The Complete Idiot's Guide to Geocaching from www.geocaching.com

Geocaching by Thomas Sadewasser

Chapter Twelve

Mud on the Carpet: Enjoying Family Pets

Most of us can look back on our childhoods and bring up some great memories of interactions with a beloved family pet. Remembering a loyal and gentle dog or a fluffy kitten perhaps, or even a canary or gerbil may bring a smile to our faces. Most likely you'd love for your kids to have these same kinds of positive experiences with an animal friend. But pets come with responsibilities. It costs money to have shots and for food and leashes and more. Do the benefits outweigh the negatives?

Health professionals agree that pet ownership offers benefits for all members of the family. The benefits are comprehensive, including physical, mental and emotional components. Pets provide companionship and unconditional love. They may offer protection to the family and certainly require a schedule of care that involves the entire family.

Many studies suggest that pet ownership comes with positive physical and emotional benefits including lowered levels of stress, depression and loneliness.

The Right Timing

You may want to wait to adopt a pet for the family until your children are out of the baby and toddler stages. You may need to consider when you're ready for the added expenses of feeding and caring for a pet. You'll need to research what kind of pet or pets best fit your family life. Here are some guidelines to help you determine whether or not your family is ready for a pet.

1. **Everyone On Board**

    As wonderful as pets can be, choosing one when a family member is not in favor of the move or being unprepared to care for it is a recipe for disaster. While there are numerous benefits to children who are raised with animals, there are also big responsibilities in the proper care and feeding of a pet. The entire family should embark upon this venture together.

2. **Choose Carefully**

    What sort of animal would the family enjoy most? Dogs are animals needing room to run and play. They need regular exercise in addition to daily feeding and watering. Cats need less in the way of running room, but still need places to sleep and eat without interruption. Even small animals such as gerbils, hamsters, and mice need a living space that can be regularly cleaned, and regular feedings. Who will do these tasks? Is the family prepared to spend the necessary money to buy the materials and food for the animal on an ongoing basis? What about vet expenses?

3. **Who Provides Care?**

    How old is the youngest family member? If there are babies or toddlers in the home, who will supervise when the animals are indoors with them? Toddlers may want to pull tails and play chase around the house. Who will be there to teach gentle petting of heads and to make sure animals aren't teased or abused in any way? Are your older children involved in many after school activities such as lessons and sports that require the family to be away from home much of the time? If so, who will have the time to care for the family pet? Who will care for it when the family goes on trips? All of these questions need clear answers before choosing a pet.

4. **Weigh the Benefits**

    There are many benefits of having pets in the home. Children who have animals around are learning important lessons in responsibility. Animals must be fed on a regular timetable and children taking on such a task will learn valuable lessons in unselfish and caring behavior. They'll learn to monitor their own behavior by treating animals gently and lovingly. They'll learn compassion when an animal needs their care and may even gain communication and social skills as they play with another living being. Animals provide lessons about life as they are born, grow to adulthood and even when they grow old and die. They provide a real connection to the world and children learn to respect life through observation and personal experience with them. Animals are a source of great comfort to humans because of their unreserved love and affection.

The purchase of a pet with all the necessary supplies and materials can make a wonderful holiday gift for your family. If the time is right and the whole family is on board, go ahead; make a plan that spells out all the tasks involved in adding this new member to the family. Then enjoy the fun and satisfaction of including a furry friend in your family's life.

Insect Mini-Pets: No Fur, No Fuss Science Observations

Kids love pets and families are enriched by the companionship of dogs and cats and other furry creatures. But maybe you're not ready for prime time pets just yet. If your children are old enough to observe the antics of insect pets and you want a low maintenance pet experience, an insect is the perfect choice. And, they lend themselves to prompting many science observations as you enjoy them.

In Japan and Europe it's quite common to keep insects as pets. Young children look forward to keeping and caring for crickets, katydids, mantids and beetles. The Japanese favorite is the giant Stag Beetle. Pet shops provide bamboo cages and other habitats plus the food items necessary for their care.

What are your choices? Well, there are many insects readily available at your local pet shop or from online distribution websites. I've steered away from spiders although many think they are fantastic pets. Spiders come with the ability to bite and some are venomous. Still, if you're the adventurous type, you can go out in your own back yard and capture a pet to keep for a time before releasing it back into nature. Or, pick up a tarantula at the pet store: lots of kids love them for their "creepy" value. But here are some other choices.

Mantises

Mantises are predators and require other live bugs as a food source. They will eat flies, moths, crickets or cockroaches. Preparing the living environment is simple: Just use an aquarium with a mesh cover, place natural objects such as twigs, rocks, soil or sand inside and be sure to have at least one twig that reaches the top of the aquarium for molting time. Mantises can be held gently. They like high humidity so mist daily with a spray from a water bottle. Mantises have a short lifespan—six months at the most.

Ants

We all know ants are industrious little creatures. They are fascinating to watch as they go about their work. There are the traditional ant farms in which dirt is the medium or the newer types of containers in which gel allows for easier observation. Some of the gel farms are illuminated with LED lights in various colors for a striking ant home presence. Ants eat seeds, pollen, sugar and some eat other insects. The usual variety of ant in store-bought farms is the Harvester Ant. These are vegetarian and can be fed with grain or seeds. Small crumbs of bread or biscuit will give them the sugar and fat they need. The gel ant farms require no feeding as there is food in the gel.

Butterflies or Moths

It is great fun to purchase butterfly or moth cocoons and then wait in anticipation for them to hatch. The cocoons require a wintering period of time before they will begin the hatching process. Most will hatch in May or June.

Beetles

Beetles are lively insects and a good pet choice for the beginner. You can purchase a jelly product for food or supply small bits of fresh fruits and vegetables. Beetles like places to hide in their environments and most prefer a sandy, dry flooring. They come in a variety of colors and sizes. Two favorites are the warty ground beetle which eats snails or the black death beetle, named for his habit of "playing dead" when disturbed.

Walking Sticks

Walking sticks come from the order Phasmida and are known as phasmids. They rely on camouflage for their defense against predators. They're one of the easiest pets to keep as they need only brambles such as blackberry canes kept in a container of water and they're happy and well-fed. There are many species of walking sticks and they're fascinating to watch.

Insects are inexpensive, easy to care for, quiet and make no messes. They're ideal pets to keep for a relatively short period of time to begin teaching your child the habits necessary for caring for larger and furrier family companions. Find insect pets at your local pet store or at one of the following websites.

www.BugsinCyberspace.com

www.antfarmcentral.com

www.petbugs.com

Making Observations and Asking Questions: Observe Your Pet

Boost your child's basic science skills of observation and data collection using this simple process.

- Gather a journal or homemade booklet, pencils, colored pencils or crayons and a magnifying glass.
- Spend a set amount of time from five to ten minutes to simply observe your pet. What do you see?
- Date your entry and write or have an adult write about:
    - Any movement observed
    - Interesting body parts of your pet
    - Creature interactions
    - Changes over time
    - Anything surprising or interesting
- Jot down any questions you have for further research.
- Draw a picture of today's observations.

Repeat this process several times a week and note changes. This is a good time to introduce simple graphing skills.

Best Kid Books on Insects

- *Children's Guide to Insects and Spiders* by Jinny Johnson, Simon and Schuster. Contains detailed information with lots of facts and full-color photos. For ages 7-10
- *Big Book of Bugs* by DK Children. Lots of buggy facts and figures with larger than life photos. For ages 5-8
- *The Best Book of Bugs* by Claire Llewellyn. Information on life cycles and habitats, beautiful illustrations. For younger readers, ages 4-8
- For your budding artists: *How to Draw Insects* by Barbara Soloff Levy, Dover Publications. For ages 5-10

Resources:

www.si.edu - The Department of Systematic Biology, Entomology Section, National Museum of Natural History.

www.BugsinCyberspace.com

"Science Skills: Making Observations and Asking Questions Like a Scientist." www.squidoo.com

Chapter Thirteen

FAMILY PROJECTS: LEMONADE STANDS WITH A TWIST

When I was about eight years old I decided it would be fun to live in a travel trailer. Our family didn't happen to own one, so I set about building one for myself. I dreamed about parking it on the very back treeline of our property and living there, wild and free.

I was a logical child so I started at the beginning. A trailer stood on wheels—I'd have to make those first. I found an old saw and some plywood and began trying to saw in a circle. It wasn't easy, but I hacked out some circle-like things and moved on. Next I'd need the floor of the trailer. I found some two by fours, nails and a hammer and pounded them together in ninety degree angles. So far, so good.

Then something unimaginable happened. My nasty older cousin came for a visit along with my aunt and uncle. He found my project and not only made fun of it, he tore it apart. I was already beginning to have some self-doubts about my progress, but his ruining my efforts sent me into angry wails.

And here's the important part for parents: My mom didn't back me up. She had no idea about my hopes and dreams. She didn't ask what I'd been building. All she saw was a little heap of wood. She told me I was being silly and to stop making such a fuss.

I was heartbroken. My dreams of living in my cozy trailer had gone up in smoke. What's the lesson for all well-meaning parents? Ellen Galinsky's book, Mind in the Making, talks about encouraging children to take on challenges. It's an essential life skill. She encourages parents to support their children when they want to build a lemonade stand, build a fort on the back forty or run in a 5K race to raise money for a good cause.

Why? Because whenever a child is willing to step out and try something, our role as parents is to cheer them on. Children don't always have the words to express the reasons they want to try something—they just know the dream is there and they want to give it a go.

Please, encourage them. Whenever possible provide the tools they need to succeed. Believe in them. So what if they only make ten cents at their lemonade stand and the sugar cost a dollar? So what if they're only able to build the wheels of the trailer? They'll do better the next time and there will be a next time with your encouragement and support.

Learning About Money

One of the most important skillsets you can give your children is a sound understanding of money. "Money doesn't grow on trees." "Do you think I'm made of money?" "We can't afford it." Does any of this sound familiar? Parents know they need to teach their children the value of money, but may not know where to begin.

Learning the basics of money management—saving and spending, planning and budgeting, is essential. Teach your children step by step and tailor the lessons to their age and understanding.

For the Little Ones

By about the age of five or six, when most children still believe the Tooth Fairy is real, begin teaching basic facts about money. Teach children to recognize and identify coins. Teach them to count money then decide if there "is enough" and make simple purchases. Teach them to make change. Teach them that nothing in stores is free and most importantly; teach them they must wait sometimes and save their money before having enough to buy a larger item. Even at young ages children can begin to learn the important concept that money is earned. They can do chores to earn their allowance.

Build Their Understandings

By the time children reach the ages of ten or eleven they're ready to understand the value of longer-term planning. They can create a budget, begin a savings account and learn to give a part of what they earn to faith-based institutions or charities. They will learn the larger concept that money management is a life-long responsibility. Saving and spending wisely will be rewarded in their adult life. They can set goals for saving up for a bike or a summer camp.

Almost Grown

Teens are often working and earning a part of their spending money. They need to take money matters seriously. They should be saving toward their future education and learn concepts of investment. They should be responsible for a portion of their clothing, gas money and other items necessary for their daily life. They should know about credit and interest, and how taxes affect their earnings. They should know how to keep a checkbook or track their spending online. By the time they're ready to leave home they should be able to make wise money decisions.

How to Get Started

As with any body of knowledge, money management must be taught bit by bit. Here are some ways you can begin training your children in this most important skill:

- Become the bank for your children. Teach them to leave part of their allowance in the bank to earn interest.
- Give out loans and charge a modest rate of interest when they want to make a larger purchase.
- Or, help them to map out the time it will take to save for a larger item. Celebrate when they achieve their goal.
- Give children jobs to do to earn extra money.
- Talk about the difference between needs and wants. There is a huge difference.
- Set up pretend stores, restaurants and the like and practice using money to purchase items.
- Play board games that require the use of pretend money.

Children learn by doing. If they have real-life or simulated experiences in handling financial matters they'll be much better prepared when it's time to make those decisions on their own. Wise use of money is a major life skill. Pass it on to your children. It may be the best gift you ever give them.

Board Games that Teach Money Management Skills

Financial Peace, Jr. by Dave Ramsey for ages 3-12
Money Bags by Learning Resources for ages 5-8
Cash Flow for Kids by Rich Dad for ages 6+
The Allowance Game by Lakeshore for ages 5-11
Pay Day Game by Winning Moves for ages 8-12
Easy Money by Winning Moves for ages 8+

Building Leadership Skills

Children often have greater thoughts, emotions and desires than they're able to put into words. They feel for the poor, the lost, the broken. But how can they help? Some children are confident enough to plan their own projects to do their part to alleviate the pain of our world, but most need a nudge or a helping hand to get going.

Kid-run Projects

A friend's daughter gave some of her allowance one year to help buy a chicken or goat for a needy family in a third world country. The following year she told her mother, she "wanted to buy the whole farm." That meant she wanted to raise over $2500 to buy a group of animals for a village. At first glance, this was just too big a project. But this wise mom asked her daughter what she had to offer in terms of raising money. Well, she could draw well. And so it was that she created Christmas cards to sell to friends, family and all-comers and she was able to give the gift her heart desired to give.

This project wouldn't have happened if the parents had dismissed the idea with "That's too much." Or "You can't do that, why not try something smaller?" Big ideas can come to fruition with the proper family oversight.

Let your kids dream and be willing to support them when they come up with admirable ideas and plans.

Kids can:
- Make and sell food and drink items.
- Do jobs around the house or around the neighborhood.
- Create artistic or craft items to sell.
- Wash cars, mow lawns, work in gardens and do other specialized jobs.
- Babysit.

- Dog sit, walk dogs or feed animals for others.
- Very responsible kids can tutor others in various subjects.

Volunteerism

In Your Own Neighborhood

When children get excited about wanting to donate to a cause, they're willing to do all of the above jobs for money with the hope of giving it away. That's admirable and worthy of your support. All of our children need to know there are others who have less and could use a little help.

And maybe there's an elderly neighbor who could use a visit, help with grocery shopping, yard work or someone to read aloud to him or her. Your encouragement to see the needs of your own community will open your children's eyes and hearts to ways they can help.

At Local Shelters, Food Banks, Soup Kitchens

With your support, your children can be part of a team of family, friends, co-workers, or church members who go out into the community to serve. Helping to serve a meal and pass out water bottles can be done by children of all ages.

Sharing a few gifts at holiday time or making useful items such as hats, scarves, or putting together gift bags with snacks, socks, etc. are wonderful ways to get children involved in volunteer work.

Nationally

Giving to Good Causes

There are many opportunities these days to run for a cure for cancer or heart disease. There are ways to work hard to raise money via jogathons, runs, bike rides and the like to raise money for a certain cause.

This sort of project is especially meaningful to your children when your family knows someone with the same health concern.

Plan an International Family Project

Want to draw your family together in a "team effort?" Want your children to grow in compassion for others? To dream big and set measurable goals? To experience the wonderful feeling of accomplishment after a lot of hard work? You'll gain all this and more if your family makes the commitment to take on an international family project.

We live in a global society. Daily news enters our homes via television and other media. Our children learn at an early age that there is war, violence and strife in many parts of the world. Most children are horrified when they learn that children around the world suffer from lack of housing, nutritious meals and a safe living environment. The reality cuts right to their heart and they want to take action.

The good news is there are tangible ways to involve children in making a difference. Can they change the world and fix all its problems? No, but they can learn the important lesson that each person has the power to make a difference, one act of kindness at a time.

There are thousands of organizations doing good work around the world. Many of them focus on the needs and welfare of children. The three I've outlined below are just the tip of the iceberg, but each of them offers practical ways to aid children in other parts of the world. Go to www.charitynavigator.org to find out more about selecting reputable organizations to link arms with.

If you decide on child sponsorships, be certain that the organization you select has procedures in place to assure the child actually gets the benefit of the gift. Choose organizations with a high rating in terms of dollars donated and dollars actually given in aid. It's fair to expect these organizations to have some overhead costs. Some sponsorship programs allow pictures and letters to go back and forth, enabling your family to get to know your adopted friend.

As you work with your family members to select a project, be sure to allow the children to "buy in" to the choice. Most organizations have excellent websites where you can research their projects and see photos of their work. In this case pictures actually *are* worth a thousand words.

Once you've selected a project with a specific goal, you'll need to find a way to meet that goal. Will you choose to do a crowd funding campaign? Will the entire family pitch in to do extra work of some kind to earn money? Will you make flyers, have a bake sale, do a garage sale?

It's not so much the amount of money you send to meet the needs of others, it's the journey you'll take together to work hard to help other human beings. That's a valuable, educational journey to make together.

Be sure your children:

- Help select the project and make a timeline (beginning and endpoint.)
- Help plan the ways to raise the funds.
- Help with advertising and promoting the project.
- Work like crazy on the fundraising days or at the events.
- Help to track progress along the way and readjust plans as necessary.
- Help evaluate the success of the project. Graphs, charts, or reports.
- Share the progress reports with those who have an interest in the project.
- Share in the satisfaction of sending the funds to the specific

organization along with any appropriate communication.
- You might want to do a family evaluation of the project. Would you want to make it an annual event?

1. **Kusewera www.kusewera.org**

This wonderful organization, founded in 2008 by Karen Osborn, a personal friend, is based in Malawi, Africa. It is dedicated to improving the life of poor children through active and creative play. Kusewera means "to play" in Malawi. The daily lives of poor children, especially those in orphanages, are often devoid of fun and healthy activity. Kusewera has developed a community center which provides sports clinics and guided activities in dance, music and art. As of 2014 they are branching out into the Philippines. In the process of teaching healthy play activities they also teach life skills such as leadership, discipline, goal-setting, perseverance and team participation. Visit the website to see the scope of this work.

Ways to help:
- Plan a volunteer trip in which you would help conduct activities with local children.
- Raise funds or donate gently-used sports equipment or gather music and arts and crafts items.
- Gather new and gently-used shoes for local children.
- Donate to the school book program.
- Check out the new pen-pal program or participate in the middle school or high school club program.

2. **Pearl S. Buck International www.pearlsbuck.org**

This organization was founded by the board of the Pearl S. Buck foundation. Their goal is to foster exploration and appreciation of other cultures around the world and to foster better lives for children. The center is based at the original family home of

Pearl Buck in Perkasie, Pennsylvania. Programs include ways to enrich the education, health and well-being of the children. This organization works in Korea, China, The Philippines, Taiwan, Viet Nam and the U.S.

Ways to help:

- Raise funds for a special project such as the restoration and renovation of an elementary school in Thailand or the Filipino Nutrition project.
- Sponsor a child. Children living in single family homes, orphans, or those in ethnic minority groups are selected for sponsorship programs. You will be the child's only sponsor and can exchange pictures and letters over the years.
- Take part in a language immersion trip planned and overseen by Pearl S. Buck International.
- Visit a summer culture camp.
- Join a high school leadership program.

3. **Palestine Relief Fund www.pcrf.net**

The Palestine Relief Fund (PCRF) is a non-political, non-profit, organization dedicated to healing the wounds of war, occupation and poverty. It works with adults and children in the Middle East and treats them regardless of race, nationality, religion or gender. They have both medical and humanitarian aid projects ongoing.

How to help: Since most of this organization's work is done by volunteer medical professionals, the best way to help is to raise funds for a specific project.

Raise funds for:

- wheelchairs
- eyeglasses
- shoes

- hearing aids

Fund
- children's summer camps
- sponsorship of a child

The organization is currently working on special projects in Gaza and Syria.

4. **Kiva**

Kiva is an international non-profit organization offering small loans to third world individuals. Using paypal they advertise loan requests, facilitate getting the money to the individual and oversee the repayment of each loan. Loans are usually given in small increments of $25 and when that loan is repaid, the donor often offers the same amount to a new recipient. Thousands of small business enterprises have been made possible through Kiva.

Be assured that when you take on a project such as supporting one of the above agencies or another like it, your entire family will be forever changed. The four non-profits listed above are just samples of ways your family can enter into the great joy of meeting the needs of those less fortunate. Your family will enjoy the feeling of uniting in a worthy cause and your kids will be eager to help determine the next family project.

Also Available from Homegrown Publications

Parents, you want your child to succeed in learning. That means learning to read. But what can you do when your child struggles with reading skills?

A lot!

You'll find answers in this book. *Homegrown Readers* will help you gain the skills you need to do and say the right things when your children get "stuck." As you apply the principles in *Homegrown Readers*, you'll see your child gain confidence in both oral reading and reading comprehension.

Available at Amazon.com | Barnes & Noble
www.JanPierce.net

www.ingramcontent.com/pod-product-compliance
Lightning Source LLC
Chambersburg PA
CBHW070626300426
44113CB00010B/1673